D1328807

Other counties in this series include:

DEVON
MURDERS

Paul Harrison

COUNTRYSIDE BOOKS
NEWBURY, BERKSHIRE

First Published 1992
© Paul Harrison 1992

All rights reserved.
No reproduction permitted without
the prior permission of the publishers:

COUNTRYSIDE BOOKS
3 Catherine Road
Newbury, Berkshire

ISBN 1 85306 210 3

Cover design by Mon Mohan
Produced through MRM Associates Ltd., Reading
Typeset by Paragon Typesetters, Queensferry
Printed by J.W. Arrowsmith Ltd., Bristol

0684332   364·152 3 H

For Lesley and Brian Warwick

I hope it was worth waiting for.

Acknowledgements

As a crime historian and author I like to feel that I do not forget anyone who has ably assisted me with their contributions, comments or criticisms, and on this occasion I am again pleased to say that I have a number of acknowledgements to make; in particular to Liz Oram, Brian Estill and C Leggatt of the Devon and Cornwall Constabulary, whose assistance was considerable, especially with my constant requests for further data; Lesley and Brian Warwick for information supplied upon the John (Babbacombe) Lee case, many thanks, you were an inspiration; the staff of Plymouth, Torquay and Exeter libraries; Mark Harrison, my young son who plagued me for goes upon the typewriter and who tapped in a number of sentences; and finally the dozens of good people of Devon who supplied so much interest and recalled so many memories that the research for this work was a pleasure to carry out. I thank each and every one of you. Finally I must not forget all at Countryside Books who once again showed great support and crafted the completed manuscript.

Contents

WITH MALICE
AFORETHOUGHT

MURDER, the unlawful killing of one human being by another is, whichever way you look at it, an emotive subject. It is an irrefutable fact of life that we all enjoy a good murder, not in the physical sense you understand, but as objective outsiders. If you disagree with this claim then perhaps you should recall just how many of those television amateur detective programmes you take in. Like it or not, murder has forced itself upon society and is an accepted part of life (or death). However, unlike the television dramas which tend to glamorize this heinous act, murder is generally a straightforward affair with the victim knowing his/her attacker in an area in which the investigating authorities examine initially.

Devon, a county synonymous with picturesque landscapes, attracts countless visitors each year who come to savour its beauty and to relax with tea and scones and fresh Devon cream. There are places within Devon which seem to have been untouched by the passage of time; places where one can forget the 20th century and all of the pressures associated with it and enjoy surroundings which have remained the same for over a hundred years or more.

Devon is one of England's few counties to possess a north

Taking advantage of the isolation and the forbidding surroundings, there has been a prison on inhospitable Dartmoor since 1809.

and south coast, with the Bristol Channel to the north and the English Channel to the south. The county is somewhat remote from the often congested inner pastures of England and has therefore sometimes been a source of refuge for the fleeing criminal; but that is not to say that it does not possess a mysterious history of its own. Indeed, Devon has a most sinister past and has suffered its fair share of tragedies through the criminal community.

The roots of today's law enforcement go back to 1324

when the 'magistrate' system became statute, although the system itself dates back to the days of Richard the Lionheart. The 1324 statute ordered: 'that within every county there shall be assigned a good and lawful man to keep the peace'. The 1361 Justice of the Peace Act collectively clarified the powers of such officers and thus indicated the way forward for law and order in England and Wales, as the magistrates were supplemented with subordinate officials known as 'Parish Constables', a system which continued for over 500 years. The police force as we know it today grew from the actions of a Bow Street Magistrate in 1763, when John Fielding succeeded in the formation of an elite group of law and order officials known as 'The Bow Street Foot Patrol', which then consisted of just ten men. The interpretations of Fielding were taken one step further in 1829 by the then Home Secretary Sir Robert Peel, who had analysed and researched all aspects of law and order and attempted to improve everything from prison conditions to practical policing. Peel had initially tried to introduce a national police force but met with many obstacles, not least the objections by county authorities, of which Devon was one of many. However, Peel introduced the Metropolitan Police Act of 1829 and firmly established the term 'police'.

When Peel progressed to the position of Prime Minister he faced mass rioting in numerous counties over the Corn Laws, termed the 'Bread Riots', a situation which gave Peel and the policing authorities many problems. The riots in Torquay saw approximately 232 persons dealt with by the local courts; two suffered transportation for a ten year period, a further six were to spend the following seven years in prison and 64 persons found themselves jailed for a twelve month period. Many of those jailed were reasonable citizens who found themselves caught up in the protests. It was a similar picture all over Devon and numerous arrests were made in Crediton, Morchard Bishop and St Thomas.

Devon, like many other counties, was a popular area for the crimes of notorious highwaymen, due to the high percentage of travellers who passed through the county en route to major towns or cities elsewhere in England. The secluded highways on remote moorland meant uninterrupted challenges could easily be made, yet many of the highwaymen from the county elected to carry out their activities elsewhere. London in particular offered the ideal prospect of wealth and a large population into which the highwayman could disappear after his crimes. A certain Thomas Gray, son of the Exeter hangman, recorded his dealings with crime and life in general in the mid 17th century, giving a marvellous insight into life during that era.

Gray's father was not only the Exeter hangman, he was also a barber of the same city who provided as much as he possibly could for his family, especially Thomas, who was sent to Oxford to learn academic skills. Whilst there Thomas earned various nicknames, such as Lord of the Razors, Little Trimmer or Young Soapsuds. He studied art and was fairly successful during his period in the city, though he had a tendency to socialise with somewhat undesirable characters who no doubt influenced him. Having left Oxford, Gray inherited some small wealth from the death of his father and then his uncle. He opted to visit London in order to spend his wealth but met with trouble on Hounslow Heath when he was confronted by a highwayman. Gray was robbed of everything and pleaded with the villain to return some cash in order that he could at least afford to stay in the capital for a time, whereupon the highwayman took pity upon him and offered to return 15 shillings in return for Gray's horse which was duly handed over.

This incident appears to have made a great impact upon Gray, who once in London fell in with a group of thieves, one of whom he describes in the following manner; 'A grave demure man, who looked like a saint. His business was to go about the streets and sell little books of prayer and hymns. He had always some text of scripture ready to vindicate what he said. He was thought to be a very holy man by the vulgar, and by this device got good store of money. If in his walk he chanced upon an open door, he went in with a great deal of confidence; if he found no one within, or if they were asleep, he never came away empty handed.' It seems that Gray was trained by members of this gang to steal. However, it was not long before one member was apprehended during the commission of such a crime and whilst in custody confessed the names and locations of all the other gang members who were duly arrested. This of course included Thomas Gray. Amazingly, Gray was not punished for his part in the gang's operations; his naivety and good character caused him to be released without serious punishment.

Gray had received a real fright and decided to leave London for a short while, but whilst away he met with another man who was like himself in many ways, particularly in his naive view of crime. Richard Brown held similar ideas of obtaining great wealth by virtue of others' losses and together the men returned to London with what little finances they had between them. Curiously, they met with another highwayman whilst en route to the capital and were again robbed, though on this occasion the event had a more direct consequence. Gray and Brown sold some of their clothing and, with the proceeds, purchased a brace of pistols for use in crime. Near Barnet they ambushed a coach in which an old man and his daughter were travelling. The duo drew their pistols and took around £40, a brace of watches and a silver snuff box from the coach passengers, and before leaving the coach Thomas Gray for no real reason shot dead one of the horses, which infuriated the old man, who called him a murderer and proffered other accurate insults. Brown and Gray rode off well pleased with themselves, though their pleasure must have turned to bliss when they found within the silver snuff box a diamond ring, which they sold and received £93 for! Gray's actions during the commission of this crime proved him to be a cold and callous criminal, he had no reason to shoot a defenceless animal which posed no threat to him or his escape. The power and status which he enjoyed whilst brandishing a pistol must have excited him greatly.

Together the men held up a number of coaches and were rewarded with various amounts of loot, which on each occasion was squandered. Eventually the pair were almost caught, when upon challenging another traveller they were shot at by his servant who summoned the assistance of other local people who at once gave chase. The pair escaped but vowed to cease such dangerous activities, especially in London. Moving to Bath, Brown and Gray heard of two wealthy sisters, both of whom were available for marriage – and sure enough they were soon convinced by the sincerity of Brown and Gray and duly married them. Shortly after this the girls inherited great wealth and thus provided the rogues with financial stability and a luxurious lifestyle for as long as they could maintain the charade. At this point Gray ends his memoirs by stating that he enjoys his easy life and thus repents his former follies!

A more farcical tale of a Devon highwayman came about in the early part of the 18th century, 1718/1719 to be precise. Nicholas Horner was the youngest son of the minister of Honiton. He had always been a difficult child with a mind of his own, yet his father displayed great patience and confidence in him. The minister supplied everything a young man of the time could require and the boy received excellent schooling and wanted for nothing. Through contacts he was able to find employment for Nicholas as clerk to an attorney in Lion's Inn, The Strand, London. However, once away from the constraints of home life Horner began to display an alter ego. He spent a great deal of time in taverns and whorehouses, the passion for work left him and he elected to run away from his employers and to lead a lazy life revolving around drunkenness and whoring. Once he had wasted all of his savings he was encouraged into a life of crime by those with whom he socialised. He procured a pair of pistols and took to the highway, resulting in instant arrest as his first attempt at robbery failed. Horner was held in Winchester gaol awaiting trial and remained there for a period of three months. Upon being brought to trial he was sentenced to death and must have repented that he had so badly ignored his father's advice.

Upon hearing of his son's fate, Horner's father created great interest in the case until it reached the ears of Queen Anne, who having listened to the minister's story, granted an official pardon under the condition that Nicholas Horner be transported out of Her Majesty's dominion for a period of seven years. Horner's father again attempted to have this punishment negated but failed to do so. Nicholas Horner was sent to Varujayati in the East Indies. After a seven year period he returned to England to find that both his parents had died and had left him an inheritance of some £500. Horner failed to learn from his experiences, wasted the cash in a few months and returned to crime on the highway.

One of his first encounters was with a farmer who was extremely low in spirits and who told Horner how his wife had become an evil spectre haunting him day and night with her wicked tongue. He could, he said, find no rest from the viperous tongue of the woman who had once been his sweetheart. Horner gave the farmer the audience he required and proffered advice upon how to deal with his problem. The farmer felt much more content once he had expounded upon his troubles to someone else and elected to treat Horner at the next inn they came to. Having consumed a few ales both men emerged from the inn and mounted their respective horses. The farmer was about to bid Horner farewell when the latter produced a pistol and thrust it into the farmer's chest and demanded money for the advice given. The poor farmer was at a loss for words and duly handed over his money pouch, which Horner snatched and rode off with, no doubt leaving the farmer somewhat bemused and irate!

Horner continued his life of crime and numerous persons suffered from his attentions, including a young couple who were en route to Henley on Thames to be married. Horner held the couple up and stole all their money and the intended wedding ring. Before leaving them he again offered words of advice, this time explaining that the couple should not wed as life was much merrier for single people. Encouraged by his success, he then stopped a coach making its way to London in the area of Braintree. The eagle-eyed coachman spotted Horner lurking in the distance and called to his single female passenger (who was a lady of considerable wealth) to hide her valuables as he suspected that they were going to be 'held up'. Sure enough Horner approached and brandished his pistol at the coachman, but whilst he was doing this the lady messed her hair up into such a state that she looked like a woman possessed and not the lady she was. Horner demanded her to alight from the coach and to deliver up her valuables, but instead of doing as he ordered she jumped out of the coach and clung onto his leg exclaiming, 'Cousin Tom, Cousin Tom'. She then continued to act like a woman deranged and told Horner that she was grateful that he had come to save her from being sent to Bedlam by her husband. Horner was terrified and turned to the coachman for support but the coachman agreed with the woman clinging onto Horner's leg! In an extremely frightened state Nicholas Horner rode off without casting a backward glance at the coach behind him. He was evidently shaken by this encounter because soon afterwards he left London and continued his robberies upon the highways of Devon where it was not too long before he was caught. He was duly executed at Exeter's Southgate on Friday 3rd April 1719, aged 32 years.

The policing of Devon ensured that the days of the highwayman were numbered and it was not too long before his character disappeared into legend. Sadly, crimes of a different form became more prominent, including house burglaries, assaults and murder. The Metropolitan Police had combated much of the crime problem in their territory of London, and the 'New Police', seen to be an active deterrent, could not be ignored for much longer by other districts throughout the country.

September 1855 saw the initial steps taken in formulating a county police force within Devon. Many towns already had their own police but the Quarter Sessions of October 1856 dictated that a single chief constable should be appointed in order to organise and manage a county force. It was decided that the position should warrant a salary of £400 per annum, added to which £200 expenses could be included, and so the position was advertised and encouraged no less than 63 candidates. Of these 16 were instantly excluded as they had omitted to insert their age, which had to be under 45 years to be acceptable by the Secretary of State's ruling, while five others were actually over this age limit, and so the number of applicants was reduced until just seven remained. Eventually Gerald de Courcey Hamilton, aged 29 and a resident of Torquay, was appointed. He had been a Sub-Inspector General of Police in Australia and had served in the Crimea.

By 1857 some 225 officers of all ranks had been recruited. Many of the junior ranks could barely read or write and may perhaps have been a little more than enthusiastic with the use or abuse of their powers. The training for these officers was almost non-existent and for those unfortunate enough to be bereft of any commonsense as well, then there were further problems. Part of a policeman's trade has to be the use of oral communication and without this an officer cannot operate in a correct and impartial manner, as can be seen from an incident which took place in Newton Abbot in 1857.

The local police officer was a Constable Winchester, and he was on patrol in the High Street of the town when he saw a cart loaded with a great amount of wood. In order to get the wood onto the cart the owner had removed the main body of the vehicle, thus removing the name which would normally be displayed upon its side (this would be similar to

Past Chief Constables of the Devon Constabulary: (clockwise) Gerald de Courcey Hamilton (1856-1891), F.R.C. Coleridge (1892-1907), Capt. H.R. Vyvyan (1907-1931) and Major L.H. Morris (1931-1946).

today's vehicle registration plate). The officer seems to have had very little good old-fashioned commonsense and so was destined for disaster before he had even started.

Winchester informed the cart owner that he was supposed to display his name upon the side of the vehicle and he then threatened to take the vehicle owner into custody for failing to do so. An altercation took place which attracted a large crowd, but despite this unwanted and unnecessary attention the officer continued the argument which had expanded to incorporate many members of the assembled audience. Threats were shouted back and forth until the incident reached such a stage that it was likely to erupt into something causing danger to those involved. Winchester then arrested an innocent man who had nothing to do with the incident and was merely going to the local pub. The man was taken by Winchester to the local lock-up. This inflamed matters and a riot almost ensued, indeed had it not been for the timely intervention of the local magistrate who released the man on bail, then without doubt serious harm would have befallen the police constable.

The subsequent trial saw the magistrate support the officer in the execution of his duty and powers, but he abstained from his support in the arrest of the prisoner, who had committed no offence! Furthermore, Winchester and those present at the trial heard the magistrate inform the court that it was his intention to write to the Chief Constable of Devon and to inform him of the facts surrounding this case. The case against the defendant was dismissed, and one must imagine the career consequences suffered by Constable Winchester.

The Chief Constable instigated the compilation of a number of rules and guidelines for police officers within

Devon. If these guidelines were adhered to then no officer would render himself liable to injury or possible prosecution, but those who dared ignore them did so at their own peril. Some of the rulings seem somewhat ridiculous but were introduced by de Courcey Hamilton in order to promote the professional image and standing of police officers. They also bred a pride in the uniform and profession. One such rule was introduced on 30th May 1860 and stated: 'Off duty officers going on leave smoking in railway carriages. If any officer is reported for such misconduct then a suitable punishment is to be administered in order to remind him that a Constable is the last person who should infringe the law'.

Sadly, the circumstances under which police officers were now operating were highly volatile and stressful. Violent crimes were on the increase and many officers were being injured or even killed during the execution of their duties. In the evening hours of 21st December 1882, for instance, a situation arose in the streets of Honiton where the recently formed Salvation Army were to hold a meeting and march through the streets. In anticipation of trouble extra police officers were drafted into the town. As the members of the Salvation Army turned into the High Street they were met by a group of anti-Salvationists, albeit Christians, and quickly a vociferous confrontation erupted into a pitched battle. Stones, sticks, in fact anything, were thrown at the police and the Salvation Army by an estimated crowd of 2,000 or so. One police officer received dreadful facial injuries as he was struck by a heavy projectile flung by the angry crowds, and countless others were to receive minor injuries. Finally, the procession made its way to the Town Hall which was packed to capacity. Further outrage ensued within the hall and a pistol was discharged, whereupon the police cleared the hall and dispersed the crowds. The police had become the first line of attack for any protesting group or organisation and have continued to be such targets ever since. It was little wonder that in 1868, some 14 years prior to the outrage at Honiton, a constable faced with a similar situation but with no assistance deserted his beat in Colyford, and when questioned by his supervisors, feigned illness as an excuse. As a result of this tragic loss of confidence the officer was branded a coward, fined ten shillings and dismissed from the force!

Yet one cannot cast all police officers in the same mould, for in 1876 the most remarkable piece of bravery to occur within the Devon force up to that time occurred. Police Constable Tucker had in his possession a warrant for the arrest of a girl, charged with theft. Knowing of her whereabouts Tucker went to make the arrest, but the girl fled and was followed by the officer. In order to avoid arrest the girl leapt into the Exeter canal. Unable to swim she began to panic as the water engulfed her. Tucker plunged in after her and attempted to save her. Unfortunately he too was a non-swimmer and lost his life attempting to save another despite the dangers to himself.

Gerald de Courcey Hamilton retired from his position in 1891 and can be congratulated for securing the foundation of a very efficient police force. Prior to his retirement in the December of that year he had introduced a detective department, which had been discussed since 1870 but at that time was deemed too expensive. Communications had also improved by virtue of the telephone and the police had welcomed improved pay scales.

Hamilton was replaced by the 39 year old F.R.C. Coleridge, who had been a district Inspector with the Royal

Ulster Constabulary. Coleridge was an excellent placator. Within his first few years in office there were several riots within the county during which the police came under attack for their apparently over-excitable attitude. Coleridge was able to explain the pressures upon his officers and the reactions of the rioters, thus giving an accurate picture of events as they occurred and defusing political arguments by objectively identifying weaknesses on both sides. During his tenure Coleridge saw the introduction of motor cars and speeding offences, he anticipated newer types of offence and issued orders to combat such problems. He had continued where his predecessor had left off and retired from the force in March 1907. Coleridge was replaced by Mr Herbert Reginald Vyvyan, a 44 year old retired captain and Superintendent in the Devon Constabulary at Cullompton.

Herbert Reginald Vyvyan did not always have an easy time during his term in office. He undoubtedly brought the force forward, leaving behind some of the Victorian values which had served its officers so well during the past few decades, and undoubtedly working conditions were to improve under his leadership. The introduction of The Police (Weekly Rest Day) Act 1910 saw officers scheduled for one day off in seven, an agreement which caused some concern to the management of the force as in theory it meant that more officers would be required to cover for those on rest days. Matters were not made easier when in 1911 the force had to supply 40 officers for duty in South Wales as a result of the coal strikes; the officers were detached for about three months.

In 1913 the Chief Constable received an official force motor car, the first in the force, and a constable trained to drive in order to act as his chauffeur. However, a Traffic

Department was introduced in 1930 when eleven motorcycles and five cars were purchased, though none of the vehicles exceeded 12hp! Vyvyan retired in April 1931 and was replaced by Major Lyndon Henry Morris, a qualified solicitor and governor of Princetown prison. Morris at once identified problems with police officers' living accommodation and the state of police stations, and he introduced better housing and official accommodation for the officers. He enrolled policewomen into the force in 1946. Morris was perhaps the most popular senior officer the force had at that time, junior ranks held him in the highest esteem and he was like a breath of fresh air running through the force. Sadly, he died in November 1946, but is to this day remembered for the fine achievements he made in respect to

Devon Police officers at Cambrian collieries in May 1921, detached for duty as a result of the coal strikes.

the manpower of the force during his 13 years as Chief Constable.

And at this point we end the brief insight into law and order in Devon, as this work does not transgress beyond the tenure of Chief Constable Morris. But this book is not just about successful policing. From whichever angle you look at it, murder affects a broad spectrum of society, and this book will hopefully allow you to take a glimpse into each facet of society and enjoy a brief journey into Devon's wicked past!

THE SECRETS OF
PINKWORTHY POND

PINKWORTHY Pond was the creation of John Knight in the early 19th century. It stands on Exmoor, some 1,500 ft above sea level, the highest sheet of water to be found in England south of the Pennines. Around 200 Irish navvies worked hard to excavate the basin of Pinkworthy, which covers somewhere in the region of three acres.

Until 1889 Pinkworthy was not an area which was readily associated with anything sinister, but in March of that year this was to change. William Gammon, a 50 year old farmer from Rowley Barton, situated close to Parracombe in the north of Devon, had suffered the tragic death of his wife. Some say that he never recovered from the loss, but certainly he soon found himself involved with a young local woman to whom he paid a great deal of attention, though it seems that she would not enter into any permanent relationship with Gammon. The farmer was persistent and refused to accept the refusals of the object of his desire, until matters came to a head and he was told outright by the woman that it was pointless continuing with any kind of relationship, and that marriage was totally out of the question.

The shock of rejection can cause any individual to act in a curious manner and sadly, William Gammon was unable

Pinkworthy Pond. In 1889, a neatly folded pile of clothes on its banks pointed to William Gammon's whereabouts, but left a question mark over his death.

to handle the refusal. He became moody, refusing to speak with anyone about the matter, then suddenly he disappeared. Various searches of his farmland were carried out but no trace of Gammon could be found, and there was not a clue as to his whereabouts until his pony was found close to the location of Pinkworthy Pond. The news of the find soon reached the people of Rowley Barton and an immediate search of the moor area was carried out. Gossip was rife when Gammon's clothes were found neatly folded on the banks of Pinkworthy! Suddenly the talk of the area was of comments passed by Gammon shortly before his disappearance, when he apparently told the love of his life that he 'intended to visit Pinkery'. There is nothing too unusual about such a statement but when one realises that he said this shortly after he was rejected, then one can place it into some kind of perspective.

With no trace of Gammon upon the moorland it was decided to drag the pond, but all to no avail. A diver from Cardiff made several descents into the muddy depths but could find no trace of Gammon's body. The water at that time of year was extremely cold and there was little chance of Gammon surviving on the moorland, so although it was realised that he must have drowned within Pinkworthy, there was little in the way of resources and only a few options available to the officials searching for the remains. The water temperature dictated that it was not feasible for one diver to carry out a thorough search of the pond, therefore it was decided to drain it by virtue of removing one of two plugs in the double drain pipes. The draining was commissioned to Messrs Jones Bros of Lynton who sent five men down to fulfil the commitment. There was, however, no requirement for complete drainage as it was not too long before they caught sight of the bloated remains of William Gammon.

There was an abundance of controversy surrounding the mysterious death of William Gammon, which still continues to this day. Why did he remove his clothes to commit suicide? Surely if he had been in a disturbed frame of mind he would not have had the forethought to neatly fold his clothes before launching himself into the chilly waters? Why did the object of his attentions fail to act when she knew that he was upset yet stated his intention to go to Pinkworthy Pond? Sadly none of these questions was ever examined at the inquest and Gammon's death was classed as suicide.

Just 23 years elapsed before Pinkworthy was again at the

centre of controversy and attention. Suddenly the talk of Gammon's mysterious death resurfaced, as speculation was now directed towards another suspicious disappearance.

William Stenner was a farm labourer aged 41 years. He was married with six children; to all who knew him he was a conscientious fellow with no enemies and certainly no worries, to his wife he was a loyal and devoted husband and to his children a caring father. Together the family lived at Riscombe, near White Cross, Exford.

During the summer of 1912 Stenner told his wife that he was having serious problems in sleeping, yet he claimed that he had no worries upon his mind. His wife believing it to be just a passing phase, paid no real attention to her husband's concerns. Sadly she was to regret this for the rest of her life, for whatever it was that was causing the insomnia forced Stenner to act in a most peculiar manner. On the evening of 9th August 1912 William Stenner told his wife that he was retiring to bed early as he felt physically exhausted. His wife bade him a goodnight and continued with her chores. Later that evening she looked in on her husband to see if he was sleeping soundly but was surprised to find that he was still awake, she therefore offered to make him a cup of tea and bring it upstairs. Stenner gladly accepted the offer and his wife trotted down the stairs in order to commence the makings. Just a few minutes passed before she was on her way back up the stairs to her husband's room, but to her utmost surprise she found that her husband was no longer in the bedroom. She at once searched the house but there was no sign of William Stenner. Curiously, it was impossible for him to have crept downstairs and through the door as he would have to have passed the kitchen area in which his wife had stood making the tea!

It may have been a few minutes before she realised that her husband was actually missing and no one knows what emotions must have run through her mind during those vital moments. Was it a practical joke? Or had he been kidnapped? Even worse, had he run away at 41 years of age? Mrs Stenner again visited the bedroom and noticed that the window was open, while further examination revealed that none of her husband's clothes were missing apart from a nightshirt which he was wearing when he went to bed. Assistance was summoned from the village and a search carried out, but with driving rain and cold winds lashing across the moor it was a difficult environment to traverse. Over the weeks which followed almost every nook and cranny was searched but there was still no trace of the missing man.

The tongues began to wag, and quite naturally there was again a great deal of speculation about Stenner's present location, either alive or dead. Many felt that he had a secret lover and had eloped with her, others held similar notions but felt that the husband of the secret lover had killed Stenner, though it is interesting to note that at no time during this period was anyone ever linked in a relationship with the missing man. The menfolk believed that Stenner may have incurred certain financial debts and his creditors had called them in, thus he had either flown the coop or had paid his debt with his life. Certainly there were certain factors which pointed to the latter as several rogues were known to pass through the area on a more than frequent basis. The police examined every alternative but found nothing suspicious, Stenner had quite simply disappeared from the face of the earth wearing just his nightshirt!

A more detailed search was carried out with the assistance

of Morland Greig, Master of the Devon and Somerset Staghounds and Yalden Thompson, Master of the Exmoor Foxhounds. Both these individuals had an in-depth knowledge of the topography of the moor and knew the areas which were suitable for the disposal of a human body. Through winter's worst, this pair led dozens of searchers through harsh terrain covered by deep snow and attacked from all angles by biting winds, but still there was no success. Finally in January 1913 there remained but one option, the dragging of Pinkworthy Pond. The difficulties of such an operation were recalled and thus it was decided that once again the plug should be removed and the pond drained.

The pond had two nine ft pipes in which two huge plugs made of English oak were fitted. The pipes were situated above each other on the pond side of the dam wall, and access to both was gained via a tunnel some 60 yards long and hardly three ft high in places. It was no place for the claustrophobic but the searchers were resolved to see the task through. It took almost four weeks but finally it seemed as though they had achieved their objective. The plug from the top pipe had been partially removed and the icy water began to flow from the pond. However, perhaps due to the cold conditions, the plug had somehow caused further obstruction and thus stemmed the flow of the escaping volume of water, resulting in the water level rising quite rapidly and actually attaining a deeper level than it had been prior to the operation!

The men were now curious as to how the drainage system within the pond worked. They knew that an artificial well some 10 to 15 ft in depth existed close to the wall of the dam and they had identified this by virtue of lengthy poles plunged into the ice cold water, which with all of the activities taking place had disturbed a deep layer of thick black mud from the basin of the pond thus causing the water to turn into a disgusting mire of ooze. The well and terrain above it had to be drained in order to drain the lake completely. It was not too long before three men again

In the freezing conditions of January 1913, the search for William Stenner's body led to the massive task of draining Pinkworthy Pond for the second time.

ventured down the dark miserable tunnel leading to the pipes, this time armed with an iron bar weighing some seven cwt and 29 ft in length. The bar was forced into place and once again forced the plug from its position, but as previously the plug managed to re-seat itself and stem the flow, and eight further attempts were foiled in an identical manner. An hydraulic jack was brought to the scene, which weighed some 140 pounds and was capable of raising weights up to 20 tons. This was placed on a platform as the men frantically worked the hydraulic system to raise the plug and for a brief moment it appeared that the plug was giving way. Water began to pour from the gap forced by the pressure of the jack then suddenly there was a crash, the platform supporting the jack collapsed and the trio were lucky not to have been injured as the whole mechanism came crashing down into the tunnel! Finally the platform was again erected, and this time the plug was removed from the pipe, water gushed into the tunnel and the three men rushed out onto the higher moorland to monitor the drainage.

A crowd had assembled upon the banks of the pond and all peered intently into the murky black depths of the pond, their eyes eagerly attempting to identify the body of William Stenner. For the first time since it had been created over 100 years previously, the depths of Pinkworthy Pond had been exposed to human view. However, nightfall was upon the gathered crowd and despite the assistance of torches and lanterns it was impossible to identify anything within the mass of mud and slime. Matters were further hampered by the fact that the water at the bottom of the pond did not drain with any momentum, thus creating dozens of little ponds within the basin. With success behind them, the search was abandoned until the morning.

At nine o'clock the following morning the men returned to Pinkworthy and to their consternation they saw that the area under the dam wall had remained submerged, though it was finally to be released later that afternoon, exposing the drainage system. Every area of the pond was searched in case Stenner's body had been washed beneath the quagmire which remained, but it was nowhere to be found within Pinkworthy Pond, and so two weeks later the stubborn plug which had been so difficult to remove was replaced into the pipe and Pinkworthy Pond once again filled with water.

There was more than a hint of dejection amongst the community who had believed that Stenner's remains would be found within Pinkworthy Pond and once again it was not too long before the rumours appertaining to his disappearance began to circulate. It seemed clear that he must have left the area, but for what purpose? Was it another woman or was it to escape secret debts? There was no respite for poor Mrs Stenner, who must have suffered terribly at some of the viperous comments made about her poor husband who, to the best of her knowledge, had done no harm to any person within the community. There were the usual spurious sightings of Stenner all over the counties of Devon and Somerset, but nothing with any conviction.

Release from Mrs Stenner's living torment came late one February afternoon in 1913. A farm labourer by the name of Reginald Hookway had been sent to Muddicombe to tend to some cattle. An old house and outbuildings stood just a short climb from the White Post road, only 400 yards from the house of William Stenner. The house, now a ruin, had been the site of an old mine closed many years previously and as Hookway passed one of the tiny entrances to the mine he happened to stop and peer into the deep blackness. A short distance within he could see something which aroused his curiosity. It was white and perhaps Hookway thought it to be a stray cow which had fallen into the cold, damp gloom within. Whatever his thoughts he brought a hayfork and prodded the object, when suddenly the horror of what he was actually prodding hit him. It was a dead body dressed in nothing but a white nightshirt.

Hookway ran to fetch assistance and before long a small crowd had assembled at the scene. There was a further problem with the removal of the body from its present position, since the dead person's dignity had to be preserved and the entrance to the mineshaft in which it now lay was just two feet wide behind a large rock. Volunteers clambered into the shaft and found the body to be laying in the freezing cold water which filled the basin of the chamber. The body was removed and identified as that of William Stenner, in remarkable condition preserved by the ice cold waters of Exmoor. The agonies of Mrs Stenner were all but over. She at least knew of her husband's fate but as to motive, well, that was another matter.

It will be recalled that every square inch of moorland was searched within weeks of Stenner's disappearance. Muddicombe too had been subjected to this search, in fact it was claimed that the very mineshaft in which Stenner was found had been actively searched, yet there was no trace of his body there at that time. It seems highly unlikely that any man would go out into open moorland wearing just a nightshirt, therefore an assignation with any person can be discounted. Why then, should he leave his cottage of his own accord via a bedroom window? The obvious answer has to be suicide, but why elect to leave via a bedroom window and why at night and more to the point, what was the underlying reason for such action? The other conclusion is that he was murdered and his body dumped where it was later found, but there was no evidence of violence and no known reason for anyone to carry out such an attack other than for the possible reason of debt. ·

One possibility which cannot be discounted but perhaps only adds fuel to the fire, is that Mrs Stenner may have been having an affair and perhaps she had her husband killed to free her into the discreet arms of another. After all, she would be only too aware of where had and had not been searched, thus the body could be secreted away elsewhere until it could be deposited safely within the disused mineshaft! If she had been the caring and devoted wife she appeared to be, then would she not have seen that her husband had something troubling him? Certainly it is difficult to believe that she had not noticed his depression and the strange character change which he must have been suffering on the night of 9th August 1912 when he calmly climbed out of bed and out of an upstairs bedroom window wearing just a nightshirt.

We shall never know the truth of either of these sad cases. Murder or suicide, on both counts we lack any sort of real motive, and the secrets of Pinkworthy Pond, which indirectly played a role in both disappearances, must remain.

THE WEDDING
RING MYSTERY

THE city of Exeter sits proudly on the south coast of the county looking out onto the English Channel. From the 10th to the 18th century it was one of England's busiest ports, located at the head of an excellent estuary and at the lowest bridging point of the river Exe, where the land and sea traders met. Though the often tranquil surroundings of river and canal provide seclusion to lovers and those who prefer the peace of their own company, they also provide the ideal location for undisturbed murder.

Sunday 25th June 1939 at Exeter police station was similar to other weekends, the officers on duty busy patrolling the streets or dealing with incidents reported by members of the public, while the constant worry of impending war loomed on the horizon and was probably one of the main topics of conversation. The control room officer at the station, Police Constable Palmer picked up the receiver of the telephone which had just begun to ring, introduced himself and instinctively picked up a pen in order to jot down the relevant information provided by the caller. However, this call was slightly different to those usually received, and the caller advised Palmer that a body had been found in a quiet location between the river Exe and the canal in Exeter.

Palmer recorded as much information as possible before advising the Duty Sergeant of the call and finding himself detailed to attend the scene with a colleague.

The officers had no difficulty in locating the body, that of a woman, and a message was passed back to the police station requesting the attendance of a doctor to pronounce life extinct, although there was little doubt in the minds of either officer. The unfortunate woman lay in an undignified manner; much of her clothing had been ripped from her body and some items of clothing were found close to the scene, as too was a handbag. Crowds began to assemble to view the gruesome scene and the police moved the inquisitive ghouls on, thus protecting the scene for investigating detectives to carry out their in-depth examination of the scene. Constable Palmer soon had a possible identity for the woman, for within the handbag found nearby was an addressed envelope and other personal papers. The address upon these papers was 111 Foxhayes Road, Exeter, and the name Edith Mabel Vincent.

Detective Inspector Kemble and Detective Sergeant Rowland were called to attend the murder scene and were to spearhead the investigation. The area was combed for further evidence and the body taken to the local mortuary.

Detectives called at 111 Foxhayes Road and spoke to George Vincent, a shoemender who had a business in the city's Holloway Street. He confirmed that he had not seen Edith Vincent, his wife, since 7.30 on the morning of Friday 23rd June 1939 when she had left home to go to her work at Cowley Laundry. When he had returned home from work on the Friday evening he found that she had not returned and as the hours passed he had begun to grow concerned as to his wife's whereabouts. He explained that he had gone out in search of her until some time around 3 am on the Saturday morning, thinking that she was in all probability in a drunken state and that she might have fallen into the roadwork excavations at the top of Foxhayes Road. He had checked these but she was not there. Eventually he had come to the conclusion that she must have gone to stay with her friend after the evening's entertainment.

The police were obviously aware that the relationship between George and Edith Vincent was anything but close, it also seemed clear that her failure to return home at night was a regular occurrence, but George Vincent seemed reluctant to admit this fact. There was perhaps a slight suspicion within the minds of those officers attending the scene that the dead woman had been a prostitute, but no matter what the woman was or had been, she was now dead, victim of a cruel attack. Someone had strangled her, forcing the last dying breath from her body with great might.

George Vincent positively identified the body as being that of his wife and was asked to account for his movements during that weekend, which he did to the satisfaction of the detectives. A photograph of Edith was taken round local public houses in the hope that someone would recognise her and perhaps a partner who may have escorted her. John Alfred Taylor, the landlord of the Devonport Inn confirmed that he had seen a middle aged woman in an apparent drunken stupor staggering up Fore Street with a man who seemed to be supporting her, he also noticed a man walking a short distance behind the couple. The landlord and staff at the New Golden Lion also recalled Edith Vincent being in their hostelry along with a man who they knew as Bill Witherington, who had been in the pub for several hours on Friday the 23rd June. He had been there in the afternoon and later that evening, and he had also been in the company of Edith Vincent. The police had their first suspect and suddenly the wheels of the murder enquiry clicked into gear and began to roll.

William Witherington was a 34 year old unemployed Torquay man. He had been forced to resign from full time employment in Yeovil due to his wife having been struck down by terminal cancer, and for the last 18 months her condition had worsened. The couple had three young children to raise and with his wife's illness this task had proved impossible for her, thereby necessitating her husband's support and assistance. Witherington was a devoted family man and the fact that he had to resign from an extremely well paid job did not concern him; he was far too concerned about his wife and family's welfare to allow professional problems to add further grief to their mounting problems. By Monday 26th June 1939 the detectives involved in the Edith Vincent murder case had not only identified their suspect, but they knew his exact movements and precise location. It was mid afternoon of a delightful summer's day that Detective Inspector Kemble, Detective Sergeant Rowland and Sergeant Lightfoot approached William Witherington as he was taking a sedate stroll along the sea front at Teignmouth. The promenade was full of holidaymakers relaxing in the resort's friendly atmosphere, the cries of young children enjoying themselves filled the air, courting couples linking arms basked in clouds of joy and happiness oblivious to their surroundings. William Witherington walked among this throng, he too oblivious to the fact that three police officers were closing in on him.

Detective Inspector Kemble was a most experienced officer and was acutely aware of the inherent problems which

William Witherington strolled along Teignmouth sea front on a sunny June day in 1939, unaware that he was about to be arrested and tried for murder.

existed when attempting to arrest a suspect amongst large crowds. A quiet assembly can become inflamed within moments and a straightforward arrest turn into a mini riot, often resulting in the loss of the object of attention. It had been decided that the three officers should discreetly surround Witherington allowing him no opportunity to escape. This was accomplished with relative ease and Kemble approached Witherington, who was shocked by the confrontation. The Inspector explained the circumstances to the detained man and asked him to come quietly, after all it was in his benefit to answer the questions put to him by the police. William Witherington was shown a photograph of Edith Vincent and at once agreed that he knew the woman but only slightly.

The police officers escorted their prisoner back to Exeter police station where he was questioned as to his activities over the preceding two days. William Witherington detailed an account of his movements which aroused great suspicion among those police officers who knew of it. On Friday 23rd June 1939 he had carried out his routine chores within the family home, then travelled to Exeter with the intention of visiting the National Assistance Board in order to relate the problems the family were encountering through insufficient monies being paid to them. He also intended to discuss employment matters with the Labour Exchange. He had acted as a part-time gardener in order to supplement the paltry sum allowed him by the government, but required something more secure, albeit part-time for the time being; it seemed to him that the staff at the Exchange cared little for his domestic circumstances and allowed no special privilege. As was usual he had called into the New Golden Lion and wasted what money he had with him, treating some of the local clientele to drinks. Without doubt he had consumed more than sufficient alcohol before resuming his journey to the Labour Exchange.

Eventually though, he did arrive there and at once demanded to speak with the area officer, Mr Thorn. William Witherington had done himself no favours by consuming alcohol, he had stimulated false courage but had numbed his perceptions and his brain and mouth seemed to be working separately. Angrily he demanded further money, causing a great nuisance within the Exchange. Mr Thorn refused to have any of it, he told Witherington to go home and that he would get no more money from the office. This further infuriated Witherington who then dug deep into his pocket and slammed down seven shillings and sixpence upon

Thorn's desk, exclaiming that this was all the money he and his family had in the world. No doubt Thorn felt like asking him why, if that was the case, had he visited a public house and wasted money upon drink? In an attempt to defuse the situation Thorn told a belligerent Witherington that whilst he was sympathetic to his circumstances, there was no provision for extra finances, but this brave attempt failed to make any impact upon the pathetic drunken man who refused to leave the Exchange until such time as he was given further funds! The situation continued until the police were summoned and duly attended. Witherington maintained his crusade but he was no match for the officer sent to the incident. The police officer took hold of Witherington's arm and firmly removed him from the building, allowing him to proceed about his business but not before first warning him about his future conduct. Even a drunken man knows when he is beaten and Witherington walked away.

Rather than return home he again visited the New Golden Lion where he consumed further alcohol. There he remained, pathetically assessing his circumstances in the clouded vision provided by the over indulgence in alcohol. Like so many drunks he became talkative and was somehow introduced to Edith Vincent, who identified herself as 'Ede'. The pair sat together for a short time until they were joined by a third person, a tall moustached man by the name of Jim who wore a trilby hat and was not very communicative, a fact which caused Witherington some discomfort. Eventually at around 9.30 pm that evening William Witherington suggested to 'Ede' that they go elsewhere, to which she agreed, but as they were leaving he observed a moment of intimacy between 'Ede' and Jim who seemed perturbed by the woman's actions towards Witherington. He then heard

'Ede' say 'Don't be a mug, Jim'. She returned to Witherington and escorted him outside. The couple then walked to the Devonport Inn where they sat down for another drink. Witherington was to later claim that this was only the eighth pint he had consumed that evening, but there is much ambiguity about the credibility of this fact. It was not too long before the couple were asked to leave the inn for closing time, but as they were doing so 'Ede' met with Jim in the passageway, where she handed him a bottle of beer and bid him a goodnight. The pair then bought some fish and chips and continued to stagger their way towards the canal.

William Witherington had assessed the situation and there was more than a suggestion that the woman was a prostitute. This was confirmed when he asked her 'How much?' to which he received the reply 'Ten shillings'. The deal was struck. During the next few minutes there were several pathetic attempts at sexual intimacy. Eventually Edith Vincent, who was also in a drunken state, rolled down the grassy bank thus breaking free of the entanglement, and appeared to hurt herself in the action. Her male companion found this unacceptable and stood up, dusted himself down and walked off. Edith ran after him and offered him sex at a discount rate of three shillings, but Witherington had had enough and refused to discuss matters further. He marched over the suspension bridge and into Topsham Road and then to Countess Wear where he visited a cafe, before finally returning to Teignmouth.

The enounter with Edith Vincent and his admission of being with her on the night of her death, close to where her body was found, placed a great deal of suspicion upon William Witherington, and at 10 am on Tuesday 27th June 1939 he was formally cautioned and charged with the

murder of Edith Vincent by Inspector Kemble. He denied the
charge and claimed that she was still alive when he left her.
At the quickly assembled Police Court Kemble requested a
remand of the prisoner for a further seven days in order that
full and comprehensive enquiries could be made into the
matter, and this was granted.

The Detective Inspector hardly needed to search for
evidence against his prisoner, for further damning facts soon
came to light. Mr Thorn the Area National Assistance
Officer recalled how Witherington had slammed seven
shillings and sixpence upon his desk claiming that this was
all the money he had in the world. Yet at the Peamore Cafe,
Countess Wear he had paid with a ten shilling note! The bag
found close to Edith Vincent's body contained an empty
purse, the killer seemingly removing any money before
leaving her.

This was not to be the only startling piece of evidence, for
on the night of her death Edith had allegedly been wearing
a wedding ring on her finger, yet when the body was found
this was missing. Furthermore, in the days between the
murder and Witherington's arrest he had attempted to pawn
a ring. Supported by such evidence the case against
Witherington began to take shape. He was further remanded
for trial at Exeter City assizes, the trial set for Monday 6th
November 1939.

The pressures of her husband's situation may have
accelerated Mrs Witherington's demise, but she was visited
at Torbay Hospital where she made a death bed deposition
which was to totally alter the course of the case:

'I lived with William George Witherington for ten years.
I was in domestic service with him in Golders Green,

London, about nine years ago, and just before that he bought me a nine-carat gold ring which was a little on the large side. When I opened by hand, the ring used to drop off, and William suggested that we buy a cheap ring to keep it on.

We were married at Poole, Dorset, on 6th February 1937, and my husband gave me a second nine-carat gold. ring then. One of my sons picked up a metal ring in the garden a few weeks ago, the other boy attempted to clean it in case it was gold. Somehow it got on the mantelpiece. The police have shown me another ring which is similar in pattern to the one my husband gave me before we were married. The ring that was too large was pawned with a Mr Wills in Torquay in about June 1938.

When I came into hospital on 12th June 1939, I had my real wedding ring in my bag. I gave this to my husband when he visited me because he had no money and he was going back to Yeovil. He said that he would sell the ring, but I told him to pledge it. On one occasion he gave me a gem ring and that was pledged with Mr Wills in Torquay as well.

Police officers have visited me here in hospital and asked me to try on a ring that I recognised as my own wedding ring. I refused to try it on. My husband has always treated me well in every respect and has never seen me want. We have had our quarrels, but we always made it up again, he is devoted to our children. The secretary at this hospital told me that my husband had been arrested, but I already knew he had been charged with a serious offence, I think it is for stealing rings or something like that.'

Mrs Witherington died on the 26th August 1939, before her husband had stood trial for murder.

A murder trial can be quite a long drawn out affair and not the sensational stadium of activity and excitement it is made out to be within television dramas, indeed there are but a few cases which can boast real courtroom drama. The case of William George Witherington is one such case, though the evidence was clearly stacked against him and not many thought that he would escape the hangman's noose. The Judge, Mr Justice Croom-Johnson presided over affairs.

The prosecution opened proceedings with the highly suspicious evidence of the missing money from the dead woman's bag and how after the confessed encounter with her, Witherington produced a ten shilling note at a cafe. The story of Edith Vincent's missing wedding ring promoted further argument. This was the basis of the case offered by the prosecution against the defendant, added to which he was of course with her on the night in question in the area where her body was to be found.

The defence counsel began by discussing a mysterious character who drifts in and out of the case and who was known as 'Jim'. A number of separate witnesses testified to seeing a man fitting an identical description, following the couple on the evening in question. Then the death bed deposition of Mrs Witherington was read out as evidence supporting Witherington's defence; it certainly knocked a large hole in the prosecution's case. Upon hearing the deposition the judge turned to the jury and asked them if they felt that there were sufficient circumstances to put William George Witherington in peril, if not then they should say so. However, the jury stated that they wished to hear all of the evidence. There can be little doubt that Mr

Justice Croom-Johnson felt that there was no case to answer, but the jury had other ideas.

One by one the defence witnesses testified. Bert Witherington, the brother of the accused, confirmed the story of his sister-in-law's slack wedding ring. Rose Hooper, sister of the dead Mrs Witherington, also gave evidence of the incorrectly sized ring, and she further stated that she had seen her sister wearing a different ring during the previous summer. Slowly the evidence accumulated to show that the ring which the accused had tried to pawn was that belonging to his wife and not the murder victim.

The prosecution attempted to regain the ground which they had undoubtedly lost when they revealed that Witherington had a cut on his hand when arrested, the inference being that this was caused during a struggle with the victim. However, this evidence was destroyed when the defence produced a witness who stated that the cut had been caused by a rose bush when the accused was carrying out some gardening tasks!

The case lasted just two days. The jury retired for one and a half hours and returned verdicts of 'Not guilty' to murder and 'Not guilty' to manslaughter, a decision which had not been expected by everyone present, including the police. William George Witherington then walked from the Exeter court a free man.

Was William Witherington guilty of murder, or did the mysterious 'Jim' hold the key to the riddle? Certainly, we have only Witherington's testimony to say who he was, yet he could not have known that he was being followed by the stranger in the trilby hat.

Much seems to hinge on the death bed deposition of Mrs Witherington which coincidentally provided many alibis for her husband, yet she claimed no knowledge of the real reason why her husband had been arrested. Within the deposition she said that her knowledge of her husband's arrest had been supplied by the secretary at the hospital, surely she would have wanted to know the reasons surrounding this arrest?

It might be pertinent to add that during the trial it was proved by the prosecution, and admitted by the defence counsel, that William Witherington had told various untruths to police officers and other persons involved in the case. Why should an innocent man feel the need to do so? Well, according to the defence it was because he felt guilty about going with another woman when his wife lay dying with cancer. Are these the actions of a loyal, trustworthy and totally devoted husband or were they the result of 18 months pressure of tending to the needs of a dying woman? The jury took the latter view, and we must leave it at that.

TRAGEDY AT
HATHERLEIGH

HATHERLEIGH can be found on the A386 Bideford to Plymouth road a few miles to the north of Okehampton. It is a place where one can escape the 20th century and appears hardly to have altered in over 100 years.

In the early 1900s Mary Breton spent many holidays in Hatherleigh visiting her uncle, Mr Isbell at Claremont Villa in the town. Mary enjoyed the peaceful surroundings which the town offered, the local countryside providing an idyllic environment to enhance her interest in painting. The 33 year old woman was greatly respected within the town, where she was known as 'the artist'; there can have been few who had not witnessed her concentration in the pastures around the area as she sketched or painted its landscapes. Mary was known to be a most amiable person who always had time to stop and talk to anyone in the area. Her pleasant attitude aroused favourable comments from all who knew or met her, indeed most of the local people would go out of their way to help her, a fact which such close communities are not renowned for, especially with occasional visitors.

May 1905 saw Mary return to Hatherleigh and once again she could be seen in the fields and meadows busily recreating the landscapes on canvas. She had been fortunate enough to find a location which suited her needs along the pathfield below Strawbridge and close to the river Lew. It was no coincidence that this very spot was favoured by grazing cattle who meandered to the river in order to drink, thus providing further natural interest to her painting. On Monday 15th May, Mary had been sketching this area and had only partly finished her work, so she decided to return early in the evening so that she could start afresh the following day. She informed her uncle that she would return home prior to dinner that same evening and all seemed well. However, a few hours later Mr Isbell became deeply concerned as to his niece's whereabouts; she had failed to return for dinner, which was most unusual as she was generally a most punctual individual. With the darkness of night falling Isbell spoke with his close friend, a Mr Veale, and explained his concern to him and it was decided that they should at once go out and search for Mary, who they thought might have fallen asleep somewhere.

The two men went to Mary's favourite location and quickly located her easel, still supporting the incomplete sketch, which was standing close to the river where Mary had presumably erected it. A few yards away lay the body of Mary Breton, her head and face so bloody that it was difficult to recognise her. Isbell was frantic, but it was clear to him that Mary was beyond help, her face was badly disfigured and there was no sign of life whatsoever. Curiously, both men noticed that her skirt was wet, but neither placed too much importance on this fact. The doctor was summoned and duly certified life extinct, and the body was returned to the town.

The inquest was held the following day at the courthouse

The site of Mary Breton's murder in 1905; still a peaceful spot for an artist.

in South Street, Hatherleigh before the Coroner for Dartmoor, Mr J. Prickman. The police were suspicious as to the circumstances surrounding the death but at such short notice had insufficient time to proffer any evidence or facts. There appears to have been some belief at this time that such inquests should be commenced and concluded as quickly as possible, which could easily lead to incorrect verdicts and the loss of valuable witnesses when all the evidence was not heard. This particular inquest promoted the most fanciful verdict that one could ever imagine. It was suggested that Mary Breton had been sitting at her easel when she had been charged by a cow or bullock, the injuries which she had received to the head and face having been caused by the animal's horns! In days when forensic science was unheard of it was of course possible to believe the improbable, yet surely there would have been supporting evidence at the scene had this theory been accurate, yet it seems that up to that point not one person had actively attempted to collect evidence at the scene of Mary's death. The jury were forced to return a verdict that 'deceased died as a result of a haemorrhage occasioned by injuries to the head, there being no such evidence to show how such injuries were caused'. It should be noted that at no time was it mentioned that Mary Breton had been murdered; had this been the case then a verdict of 'murder by person(s) unknown' would have been offered. However, the latter was commonly believed as being the truth of the matter by most Hatherleigh residents, indeed there were those who could even supply the name of the likely murderer!

Such rumours are common enough after tragic events, but the rumours circulating in the town were more than idle gossip. Police Sergeant Hill, the officer in charge at Hatherleigh also held suspicions about a local man. He refused to accept the verdict or theory proposed at the inquest and so commenced to carry out discreet enquiries into his suspect's movements on the 15th May.

The name on the tip of everybody's tongue was John Ware, who had returned to the town some three weeks earlier having served a twelve month prison sentence at Exeter for indecently assaulting a woman at Doddiscombsleigh. The Sergeant discovered that Ware was now in employment, working at Brimridge ripping bark. The journey to and from work would take Ware and many other men along the Strawbridge footpath and passed the area where Mary Breton's body was found; some of the workers recalled seeing Mary Breton working at her easel, thus John Ware must also have known she was there. The Sergeant's suspicions had been aroused, and increased when he learned that on the evening of Mary Breton's death John Ware had made an excuse to leave his workmates after work at Lewer Bridge, which is situated close to one entrance of the Strawbridge pathfields. His fellow workers had gone on without Ware, having left work at around 6.15 pm.

Further enquiries revealed that Ware had failed to return to Hatherleigh until around 8.30 pm on the night in question. He had been seen in the London Hotel where he lodged, where he had a pint of beer and gave the impression of being extremely nervous, his hands shaking as he accepted his drink. Furthermore it had been noted with more than a hint of curiosity that the lower legs of his trousers up to his knees were wet! Another man known to Ware told how he

The neglected gravestone of Mary Breton, as it is today.

had met with him in the churchyard; the man spoke to Ware but received no reply, in fact Ware had maintained a stare towards the ground. This was a strange route for him to have taken from his work, as he approached via a lane leading to Meeth road and not by the Strawbridge pathfields route. Sergeant Hill spoke with the owner of the London Hotel where John Ware lodged. He was informed that her lodger acted in quite a peculiar manner on the night in question. He had told a few people that he intended to leave Hatherleigh the following morning to go to Plymouth and he had remained in the kitchen area of the hotel until 1.30 am, when he was ordered to bed. The following morning he failed to go to work, a fact which coincided with Mary Breton's inquest!

On Wednesday 17th May, John Ware left his job at Brimridge and commenced work at Hannaborough Quarry. That same day he was visited by Sergeant Hill who asked him a few relevant questions which were unsatisfactorily answered, and Ware was asked to accompany the officer to the police station. Once there Hill requested the attendance of Superintendent Bond from Holsworthy, with the brief explanation that he believed he had a murderer at the police station. The Superintendent arrived within 30 minutes and listened intently to his Sergeant's conclusions. John Ware was secured in a cell as the two officers left the station in order to visit the scene of the alleged crime, Constable Smith being left at the station in order to keep watch on Ware and answer any enquiries that came in. The two policemen scrutinised the scene of Mary Breton's death and met with great success. They found evidence of a struggle with various marks upon the grassy bank, but more conclusively they located a number of stones which were smeared with blood.

Both men at once realised the importance of such a find, the stones had been used to batter Mary Breton to death!

The two officers must have been elated at the discovery of such evidence, and even more satisfying was the fact that the number one suspect for the attack was well and truly secured in the cells at the police station. The numerous questions that required answering must have been gathering in the two officers' minds as they returned to Hatherleigh police station. Upon entering however, they were surprised to be greeted by the local doctor, and shocked Constable Smith. The constable told his seniors that Ware had been in his cell for around 45 minutes, where he had been quiet and apparently subdued by his present circumstances. Smith had decided to pay a routine visit to the cell and was surprised to find John Ware on his back on the stone floor of the cell, blood running from his ears and a gash in his head. A scarf had been tightly tied around his neck. Ware had apparently stood on the bed with the scarf acting as a kind of tourniquet preventing blood from reaching his head. He had lapsed into unconsciousness and fallen from the bed onto the floor where he had struck his head, causing the wound. The doctor had examined him, pronounced him dead and confirmed death as being caused by strangulation. Sergeant Hill's man had escaped justice, but had seemingly suffered an agonising death in preference to being officially 'turned off' by a hangman.

An inquest into Ware's death was opened the following day, 18th May 1905. The evidence was overwhelming and the jury passed the verdict: 'That the deceased, John Ware, died from strangulation self-inflicted, whilst in sound state of mind. That he killed himself from fear of punishment, that the jury are of the opinion that the action of the police in

Hatherleigh Police Station, where the chief murder suspect committed suicide in a bloody and final admission of guilt.

detaining the deceased was fully justified, and that no blame in any way was attached to Constable Smith, or anyone else, on account of the death of the deceased.'

The contempt of the people of Hatherleigh for this brutal murderer was truly depicted by virtue of the fact that there was no one locally who was prepared to make a coffin for his body, and eventually his remains were wrapped in a sheet and pulled through the streets before being buried on the edge of the local graveyard!

CARNAGE AT
CULLOMPTON

C ULLOMPTON is now a thriving town situated close
to the West Country's main thoroughfare, the M5
motorway, which winds its way down from the
north, probing deep into the Devon countryside. Today the
town boasts many modern amenities but 300 years ago its
residents were mainly farming people living off the land. In
the main these were good honest people who would readily
assist a neighbour without requesting a favour in return; it
was perhaps one of the most tranquil areas within the region
and was not renowned for anything but its rural atmosphere.
Sadly, in 1694 Cullompton suffered greatly when it was
thrust from obscurity by a murderer of horrendous
dimensions, author of most certainly the saddest and the
ugliest crimes I have ever researched, Thomas Austin.

With the crime occurring so long ago it is not surprising
that the actual facts relating to the incidents of murder are
but brief; however it is not only the commission of the crime
which must cause debate but the genuine reasons behind it.
Like the best fictional crime story, just when you think you
have grasped the killer's reasoning, then he does something
totally alien to his character!

Thomas Austin was born in Cullompton to wealthy and

well respected parents who were honest hard working farmers. The Austins owned everything under their name, unlike so many who had large mortgages or encumbrances upon their property. The couple worked to provide for their family and upon their death Thomas inherited everything. Now one would expect the son of such an astute family to be more than intelligent with his newly acquired wealth, but for Thomas Austin the position was difficult. Although of a mature age he was mentally immature and had no one to guide him in the correct direction, although it has to be said that he never once accepted any advice which may have been proffered.

The general annual income from the farm was in the region of £80, which by 17th century standards was a substantial amount, thus providing Austin with the foundation of an affluent lifestyle. The social circles which Austin frequented introduced him to extremely wealthy families, many of whom had ambitions of marrying their daughters off to one of their own kind. Austin was now an eligible bachelor and found himself invited to many functions, and eventually he met with and married the daughter of a neighbouring farmer. Thomas Austin's bride had been provided with a dowry of some £800 and it appears more than likely that this fortune was one of her new husband's reasons for marriage, albeit perhaps not the sole reason. Up to this time Thomas Austin had maintained a reasonable sense of his circumstances, but everything was to alter in a more than foolish and dramatic manner. The riches now available to Austin caused a dramatic character change as his alter ego took control of his life.

Austin threw extravagant parties and quickly gained a reputation as a marvellous though somewhat financially irresponsible host. In short, he wasted major sums of money and disregarded the upkeep of his own property, allowing it to fall into a state of disrepair. Soon no profits were forthcoming from the land and it was not long before he had mortgaged much of the farm and surrounding property and had in fact incurred debts. To add to this financial nightmare Austin had twice become a father, all within four years of marriage.

Thomas Austin attempted to maintain his influence within the region, but most people knew that his riches had long since been wasted. In a vain attempt to turn over a new leaf, Austin tried to return to farming, after all he had been raised on the farm and knew much about the land. Sadly, it was too late, for farming does not produce the instant wealth which Austin required and the state of the land had deteriorated so much that it was a long term proposition to bring it back to its rightful condition. Over the months which followed Austin fraudulently obtained monies from his one-time friends and neighbours. It seems that many of these people actually forgave Austin and failed to act against him, in a marvellous display of loyalty, although one must suspect that they would hardly be willing to confess to having been duped. The sad fact is that these same people were only adding to Austin's downfall, for the longer he got away with crime the more ambitious he was to become. His adventurous spirit soon took him along the roads and highways of Devon as he took to the discreet activities of highway robbery, and to some effect as he seems to have had a good deal of success in this area.

On one occasion Austin monitored the movements of Sir Zachary Wilmot, who was known to travel with large amounts of money upon his person. Eventually Austin confronted Wilmot in the emptiness of the Wellington to Taunton Dean road, where he robbed Wilmot of the riches which he was carrying, some 46 guineas and a silver hilted sword. The gentleman attempted to recover some of his money during the confrontation, at which point Thomas Austin drew a pistol and shot Sir Zachary Wilmot dead. He then rode off with the booty and escaped detection and to some extent, suspicion.

The monies stolen during the murderous attack helped a great deal in once again substantiating Austin's position in the local community, but as on previous occasions the wealth did not last and it was not long before once again his creditors were knocking upon his door. The stress and pressures these circumstances must have placed upon the marriage, both mentally and physically, must have been enormous. It is not certain whether Austin's wife knew of his criminal activities, although it seems highly unlikely that she would not have held suspicions about the origins of the money and articles brought home by her husband. Whatever her opinions, they were seemingly kept to herself as she did little to prevent her husband continuing with his life of crime. She had to provide for her two tiny children, and after all it was not her business to question her husband, he was the provider and that was all she required to know.

It was not too long before Thomas Austin returned to the highway and a life of crime, a life which was causing him great internal misery. In 1694 Thomas Austin's brain seems to have finally given way. Home matters had gradually deteriorated and after an altercation with his wife Austin stormed out of the house, telling her that he was going to visit his uncle, who lived about one mile distant from his home. During that journey Thomas Austin must have deliberated over his wasteful life and upon arrival at his relative's home he had seemingly walked his temper out of his system. Thomas entered the house occupied by his aunt and uncle and their five children. He was told that his uncle was out but that he was welcome to wait until he returned when he could discuss his business with him. It is not clear whether Austin had explained his dire circumstances to his relatives, but undoubtedly they were aware of his career in crime.

A man in such turmoil must find great difficulty in maintaining concentration upon any one given subject, but just what went through Thomas Austin's mind during those fateful few moments at his uncle's house we shall never truly know, for he had hardly been there five minutes before he snatched a hatchet and drove it through his aunt's head. The blow split the woman's skull in two and she fell to the floor dead. Not satisfied with this, he then took a knife from the kitchen and hunted down the five children within the home. It is terrible to imagine just what emotions must have been running through these poor tormented souls' minds as they witnessed the cruel murder of their mother. One by one, Thomas Austin grabbed the children, who must have squirmed in his grip, and slit their throats, then he inhumanely piled the limp bodies on top of each other in a most undignified manner. One can only imagine how the children scattered and attempted to hide as each one witnessed the slaughter.

With this done Thomas Austin then went upstairs and ransacked the bedrooms until he found the object of his desire, money! He took all he could find, somewhere in the region of £60, and quite calmly he then left the house and returned home. On his arrival there he was met by his wife who at once asked why he had bloodstains upon his clothing. Austin yelled 'You bitch, I'll soon show you the manner of it!' He then produced the knife used to hack through the throats of his five tender victims elsewhere in Cullompton, and in a similar manner he ripped open his wife's throat from ear to ear. He then sought out his own two children, the oldest of whom was just three years of age. He slit their throats, mutilated their bodies, and covered himself with blood in the process.

Thankfully, before Austin had any opportunity to escape he was visited by his uncle who had called in by chance on his way home from business. The sight which greeted him must have sickened him greatly, but he at once rushed back to his own home, possibly because Austin was murmuring of a similar fate having already been met by his family. Upon finding the carnage there, the uncle returned and at once violently attacked Austin, rendering him unconscious. Once he had regained consciousness Thomas Austin was marched to a local magistrate who at once committed him to Exeter gaol, from where he was tried and found guilty of the murders of his wife and aunt and seven children. He was hanged at Exeter in August of the same year, 1694.

Just what kind of person could commit the atrocities carried out by Thomas Austin? The reader will not of course be slow to recognise the parallels with notorious cases of apparently motiveless mass murder carried out in recent years. There can be few crimes which cause such sickening revulsion to reader and author alike, but can we attempt to identify just what caused Austin to act in such an incredible manner; after all up to that point he had displayed no real signs of insanity or serious mental disorder?

There are many reasons for murder – lust, greed and

jealousy to name but a few. Today we can understand any number of pressures which can cause a person's mind to snap, thus causing potentially violent disorder and subsequent acts of murder, and all too readily use the 20th century expletive 'Stress' in order to identify mental anxieties and irregular acts. In previous years it would have been suitably titled as 'Worry'. It is not a problem of the modern age but has rather been identified as such in recent times.

So what stress or pressures did Thomas Austin have to bear? The worry of loss of social standing, the debts incurred, even the normal day to day worries of family responsibilities all added to his problems to the extent where he no longer trusted anyone, much in the same way as he knew that he himself was greatly maligned and mistrusted.

Eventually he could cope with these pressures no longer, and he murdered those closest to him in an act of defiance for their mistrust, ridding himself of family pressures – especially as they of all people knew only too well what a waster he actually was. The murder of Sir Zachary Wilmot was perhaps his first taste of real violence, and when he escaped justice he may have felt immortal and above the law, so clever that he could always outwit those whom he classed as his pursuers.

This, perhaps is as close as we will ever get to identifying why Thomas Austin murdered nine innocent people, but despite such reasons we should never lose sight of the fact that he was a cowardly killer, despatching those he knew could offer little resistance to his actions. He met his match upon the gallows, but perhaps a quick death upon the hangman's noose was a little too good for him. Certainly the final paragraph of his activities as depicted within the pages of the Newgate Calendar or Malefactors Register depicts the emotions felt at the time; 'In the month of August 1694, this inhuman wretch suffered the punishment provided by the law, which appears much too mild for such a black unnatural monster.'

ANGLIA

A CRIME OF
PASSION

PETER Tavy is located on the western periphery of
Dartmoor, a small remote community which was in
1892 reliant on the land. The parish of Peter Tavy
actually covered a fair sized area, most of which was remote
farming land with the odd smallholding situated close to
farmsteads. It could be said that the people who resided
within the parish were reasonably satisfied with their lot.
The policing of Peter Tavy during the latter years of the 19th
century was provided by a village constable who reported
direct to local headquarters at Tavistock. The officers who
covered the district had very little in the way of serious crime
to deal with, occasional drunkenness and the odd theft or bit
of damage was as far as it went, and so it must have come
as a great surprise when they were called upon to deal with
a double murder!

Eunice Holmes Doidge was the 17 year old daughter of a
local farmer who hailed from Coxtor Farm, Peter Tavy. She
was actually christened as Emma, but was known to all as
Eunice, and was an attractive young girl who was extremely
popular with most of the young men within the district. This
had nothing to do with sexual favours but was down to the
honest fact that she was pretty and good company – there

is also the possibility that she had little in the way of opposition and therefore she held a distinct advantage over her suitors. Eunice could afford to pick and choose whom she went around with and every so often she would break a heart.

Early in 1892 she met with and started to date a young man who was known as William Williams. He too hailed from farming stock and to all intents and purposes he seems to have been 'quite a phlegmatic sort of person' who was not easily excited or aroused. The relationship appeared to be of mutual satisfaction and Eunice seemed as enamoured with her suitor as he did with her; one must gather from this that there was a great amount of envy against Williams by his contemporaries. The relationship was perhaps not the kind which was taken seriously by the adult members of the community, but was viewed as more of an innocent encounter, part of the learning and maturing process. How wrong these people were to be!

Eunice Doidge eventually became bored with Williams' constant attentions. She apparently felt suffocated by him and found herself unable to make decisions without his interference. Over the following weeks Eunice attempted to avoid Williams; she feigned illness and told white lies in an attempt to bring home the realisation that the relationship was over. Yet William Williams was oblivious to the fact that Eunice wished to terminate what he saw as a close relationship, he was totally besotted with the girl and thought about little else.

Eunice Doidge took the easy option and elected to ignore his advances, and it appears that for a while she was unable to tell him directly that she wanted no more to do with him.

Indeed she refused to speak to him, to the extent that Williams began to fret. The news that Eunice had begun to court another youth within the village must have come as a great surprise to Williams, after all he had been given no reason or explanation as to why she felt such obvious animosity towards him. Suddenly this young man who had no real history of violent mood swings seemed most agitated. For many days he sulked and was sighted by various people acting in a curious manner in the country lanes in the area. He had taken to walking alone and it was believed that he often talked to himself. Friends rallied around and attempted to revive his spirits and to some extent they seem to have succeeded, the shock of rejection had apparently worked itself out of his system.

Yet William Williams was a young man in turmoil. Inwardly he was being torn apart and his love for Eunice still simmered, although outwardly he was able to disguise such emotions. By November 1892 most people had forgotten the problems suffered by Williams and life was again normal, that is, to everyone except William Williams. On 8th November of that same year he visited Tavistock and purchased a revolver and a quantity of ammunition from an ironmonger's shop. He explained that it was to be used on the land, a reasonable explanation for purchasing such a weapon, and no suspicion was raised against him. On Sunday 13th November 1892 Eunice Holmes Doidge made her usual visit to Peter Tavy church. She was in the company of Frederick Rowe, another local boy whom she had been courting for a number of weeks. Unbeknown to anyone other than Frederick Rowe, Eunice Doidge and William Williams, the latter had been making a nuisance of himself by constantly following her and requesting her forgiveness

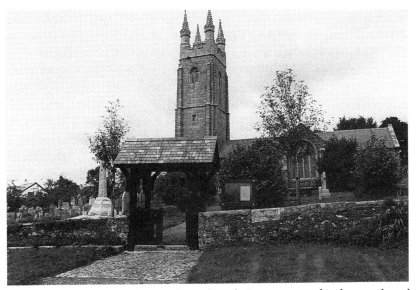

Emma (Eunice) Doidge and Frederick Rowe were both murdered near the lych gate of Peter Tavy church, shown here.

for whatever he had done to hurt her. Eunice had told him that the relationship was over and that she no longer wished to see him. Williams had openly sobbed and begged her to finish with Rowe and to come back to him but Eunice had stood firm and refused to be drawn into any further discussion upon the matter, and that was the state of affairs up to the 13th of November.

Eunice Doidge and Frederick Rowe left the church at around 9.00 pm, Rowe walking her home for the evening, when suddenly they were confronted by William Williams. The tranquillity of Peter Tavy was rocked by the loud bangs of gunfire. A bullet struck Eunice Doidge in the head, killing her outright, and another bullet entered Frederick Rowe's skull. He lingered at death's door for a few hours before finally expiring the following morning.

Witnesses leaving the church and following the same route home as the young couple were horrified as Williams turned the revolver upon himself and fired one shot deep into his neck. He then threw himself into the nearby river Tavy. The police were summoned and Williams was dragged from the river and taken to the cottage hospital in Tavistock where a bullet was extracted from his neck, thus saving his life.

The revolver was taken into police possession and examined by an expert. The bullets removed from the skulls of the two murder victims identically matched with the one extracted from Williams' neck and two further unspent cartridges which remained within the revolver. Williams was eventually brought to trial at Exeter where he was found

The gravestone of Emma Holmes Doidge (known to all as Eunice), innocent victim of a jealous rage.

guilty and sentenced to death. He was hanged at Exeter prison on the 28th March 1893.

Sadly such instances are all too common. William Williams was the victim of his own circumstances. It may well be that had Eunice explained her feelings to Williams at an earlier stage then he could have accepted the circumstances in a more mature manner, thus saving three lives. However, murder is an unforgivable act and William Williams suffered the correct punishment for his outrageous crime of passion.

THE FOUL CRIMES
OF THE REVEREND VINE

TUCKED away in the most westerly point of Devon are a number of communities which remain virtually untouched by the forces of the 20th century. The centre of this western outpost is the town of Hartland, indeed the most westerly point of Bideford/Barnstaple Bay is called Hartland Point, and one can well imagine that this region could be a separate county within itself, albeit the residents of the area are devoted Devonians. The people of this area are among the friendliest in the county – yet it contains many fine tales of murder, mystery and mayhem.

Peter Vine was born in Hartland, Devon in 1876. His parents were hard working and well respected within the region and were typically proud of their son, who through the years displayed a reasonable level of intelligence and a leaning towards the Church. John Vine, his father, was of a religious disposition and the family were regular attenders at the parish church. Just how far this religious enthusiasm went is not known but it seems likely that the family were close to fanatics and thus Peter Vine may have been raised within a restricted and authoritarian home. This style of upbringing did not at first appear to have caused him any grief, however, and his parents were exceedingly pleased and proud when he announced that he wished to pursue a career within the Church. They spent a great deal of money on providing for him in order that he might accomplish his goal, and it was not long before he received Holy Orders and was made the vicar of his home town, Hartland.

For many months the Reverend Peter Vine worked hard at preaching the Gospel to his community. He carried out regular visits to many of the homes within the area and it must be said that he appeared to be the ideal vicar. It was also to his advantage that he had good academic skills, thus making him very popular among those who could afford to pay for their children's education, though Vine also taught the less fortunate members of the community. Naturally such keenness and generosity brought him respect from almost everyone with whom he came into contact.

Early in 1811 there were a number of rumours within the area relating to the Reverend Peter Vine's apparent relationship with a Mrs Dark. Most certainly he was visiting the home with some frequency, but despite such speculations, to all intents and purposes his visits seemed to be solely upon a professional basis.

It was nothing unusual when in January of 1811 the Reverend Peter Vine again visited Mrs Dark with the purpose of teaching her eleven year old daughter. Mrs Dark was reasonably affluent and owned a pleasant home in Hartland surrounded by large gardens through which she could often be seen walking. However, during this visit to the Darks' home, the Reverend Vine was out walking in the garden with Mrs Dark and her daughter. Mrs Dark left the pair alone to continue the lesson and returned to the house. During her absence Peter Vine attacked the defenceless child, and proceeded to rape her. He then jumped over the garden wall and fled the village.

Mrs Dark was unaware of the attack and upon her return from the house was devastated by the scene which confronted her; such was her horror that she at once fainted. There she lay close to the body of her violated daughter, and it appears that she must have remained in an unconscious state for some time as a servant from the household was forced to go out into the garden in order to see what was delaying her return. The alarm was raised and a search of the village and outlying districts carried out without success, there was no trace of the Reverend Peter Vine!

Mrs Dark offered a reward of 20 guineas for anyone who could provide information as to his whereabouts in order that justice should be done. The whole village was in uproar. One cannot imagine what grief and embarrassment his family felt for his actions; it seems more than likely that they suffered greatly as a result of the incident and undoubtedly had their home searched on numerous occasions. The memory of the attack failed to drop from memory as the weeks turned into months, but still there was not a trace of Vine although various sources claimed him to be in the Barnstaple or Bideford area. There is some suggestion that he remained within the north of the county, though it would seem unlikely that he would flee to one of the major towns close to where he committed the atrocity.

Then, on Sunday 17th April 1811 the Reverend Peter Vine casually returned to Hartland as though nothing unusual had occurred. He told several people as he passed through the village that he would shoot dead the first man who should attempt to take him, and this seems to confirm that he knew of the reward placed upon his head and that he was wanted and would be hunted down. It is not known which house

Vine went to but it seems likely that he returned to his family home and there he remained.

The news of his return spread through the community like wildfire. There were claims that he was heavily armed and that he promoted the image of a man possessed. Upon learning that Vine had returned to Hartland, Mrs Dark at once visited Mr Justice Saltern and obtained from him a warrant for the arrest of her daughter's rapist. Armed with this she at once visited the home of the Hartland constable, who apparently knew of Vine's return and had summoned the assistance of two local men in order that they could overpower him, especially as rumour had it that he was armed. The two men, Roger Ashton and William Blake, both knew of Vine and probably hoped that he would come quietly, but in any case they were prepared to do battle with their quarry.

The three men approached the house where it was known that Vine had entered. Admittance to the house was barred and so the men broke open several doors until eventually they arrived at the room in which they knew Peter Vine was hiding. The lock was forced open and Roger Ashton was the first to burst into the room. He was confronted by the Reverend Vine, who held a pistol in his hand. Ashton was about to approach him but had no opportunity to do so, a loud report echoed around the walls of the house and Ashton fell to the floor, dead. Vine was given no time to reload his pistol, the two remaining men leapt upon him and disarmed him before removing him from the house and taking him before Mr Justice Saltern, where he was questioned about his actions and guilt for some two hours.

During the questioning Justice Saltern told Vine that he had no doubt of his guilt in respect of the rape and assault upon Mrs Dark's daughter; the fact that he had absconded from his duties and position in the village was most influential in determining guilt. Despite such evidence Vine refused to confess, though of the murder of Roger Ashton he had little defence to offer. The news of Vine's capture spread through the village and reached his aged father, John Vine, who at once made his way to the home of Justice Saltern where he confronted his son: 'With what a load of grief have I at last arrived, to see this dreadful sight of Infamy, and you, which cuts my very soul to see, should be the sole occasion of it. O! that I had died in my mother's womb that I could not have seen the sea of sorrow, you in whom lay all my delight and pleasure of this life, now proves the destroyer of it!' John Vine was distraught, the grief caused by his son's return and subsequent act of murder were to force him to retire to his bed where he died just ten days later.

Peter Vine was brought to trial at the Guild Hall, Exeter, on 25th April 1811 where he was found guilty of the rape of a child and murder of Roger Ashton; he was sentenced to death and the date set for Thursday 4th May 1811. During his term of imprisonment Vine constantly denied the rape but admitted the murder. He spoke to other prisoners with whom he regularly prayed and it appears earned a great deal of respect from his keepers. He arose early on the morning of his execution and received the Blessed Sacrament. He appeared strong as he walked to the gallows tree, around which a large number of persons had gathered in order to witness his execution. It seemed almost as though he was climbing into the pulpit when he ascended the gallows ladder, turned to the assembled throng and made his final speech on this earth:

'Loving people, I see there are numbers of you assembled to see me depart this sinful life, in shame, and as I am a dying parson no doubt you expect to hear something of the fact for which I suffer, especially from me who was sent as a messenger from God to instruct His people, and not to learn them more wickedness, by breaking into evil paths and following not the righteous ways.

I say as there is a fine and just God, who doth sitteth upon the seat of Judgement in Heaven, whom before I must presently appear in order to answer my sins, that I am not guilty of rape which I am charged with, committed upon the body of Mrs Dark's daughter. I confess that I committed murder upon the body of Roger Ashton, but that I stood that on my own defence, therefore I think I have the less sin to answer for, as he never told he his business when he came to take me, and I being in fear for my life and of being robbed discharged the pistol which shot him dead. As for my absconding, it was through my father's ill state on whose death a hundred pounds was depending, and who has since died through the grief of this unhappy affair. I pray God be with you all, and beg you all to pray for my departing soul, and desire you to shun all treacherous persons' company, in doing which you will do good both to God and to yourselves!'

Despite such an eloquent speech there were few within the gathered crowd who felt any sympathy towards Vine, and despite his claim as to his apparent innocence of the rape of the young child it seems obvious that he was guilty, his departure from the village bringing the immediate suspicion of guilt followed by his comments to villagers upon his return and the threat to kill the first man who attempted to take him. It would seem that the rape was an opportunist crime, brought about by apparent sexual frustration; perhaps he felt that such advances to an adult would be denied hence he took it out upon the poor innocent child.

Whilst in prison awaiting execution Vine favoured the following prayer:

'O God who hath not given laws to be traps and snares, nor on purposes that they may be broken, and poor mortals be brought under the lash of the law and be sentenced to damnation, hear me, O Lord, and have mercy upon me, for I have sinned against Thee; I heartily pray and beseech Thee, in the bowels of Thy mercy, to look down from heaven upon me Thy poor servant, whom Thou chose as a shepherd, to watch Thy flock, and whose sins be infinite and immeasurable, most heinous and insupportable, but as they be grievous without number, so is Thy mercy more abundant and without end. Turn not Thy face away from me that lies prostrate, lamenting for his sinful life before Thy mercy gate; which Thou dost open wide to those that do lament their sins; O shut it not against me Lord, when I depart this sinful world; but let me enter in, and call me not to a strict account how I have lived here. Thy mercy is above all Thy works, more able to save than my sins to condemn. Therefore, O sweet Saviour, for Thy bitter death and passion, and for the glory of Thy name, be merciful unto me, and forgive me all my sins, as I heartily repent, and the Lord Jesus Christ remain with me now and for ever more, Amen.'

Presumably, the terms 'immeasurable', 'heinous and insupportable', relate to the rape rather than the murder as he all too readily admitted that he killed Ashton in the belief that he was to be robbed or attacked. Vine realised that the crime against the young child was an unforgivable act, the product of a sick and demented mind.

Locally the crimes created much interest. Although most people deplored the Reverend's acts he became part of the local folklore and hundreds of people visited the village and the grave of Roger Ashton, removing 'souvenirs' from the church where Vine had once preached. Such was the public interest that various copies of verses relating to the crimes were distributed and sold locally:

'You tender Christians all, of high and low degree,
Stop a few moments and listen unto me,
A shocking tale you shall now hear,
Will surely draw forth many a tear.

In Hartland town, It's known full well,
The Reverend Peter Vine, he there did dwell,
Minister of that parish church was he,
Respected by all, of high and low degree.

A widow lady in the same town did dwell,
Had a daughter eleven years old, that she loved full well,
To this minister she sent without delay,
To have her brought up in virtuous ways.

Surely the Devil must him possess,
For to commit such wickedness,
On her he did commit rape,
And left her in a shocking state.

A reward was offered then with speed,
They went to apprehend him for this deed,
Soon as the room they entered,
He quickly shot one of them dead.

When at the bar he did appear,
The court with horror was filled we hear,
To see a man in holy degrees,
Found guilty of such crimes as these.

Now he's executed for the same,
Great numbers went to see him die in shame,
By this minister's fate, be warned I pray,
Never let your passions lead you astray.'

THE BABBACOMBE
MURDER

THERE can be few occasions when the aftermath of murder is more fantastic or as well documented as was the case of John Henry George Lee, otherwise known as 'The Babbacombe Murderer'. Situated to the north east' of Torquay, Babbacombe's rambling cliffs tower majestically above the English Channel and the community has always been a popular retreat for holidaymakers seeking tranquillity and relaxation. It is not the kind of place where one expects scenes of murder and mayhem, yet in 1884 Babbacombe's inhabitants were horrified by the news that the Devil himself had been at work committing murder within their close knit community.

John Henry George Lee was born in 1864 in the tiny community of Abbotskerswell which is to the north of Torquay and no great distance from Babbacombe, the scene of this awful tragedy. Lee was the son of a yeoman farmer and his wife residing at number 3 Town Cottages, Abbotskerswell. He attended the local village school and was of an average academic standard, though perhaps he had greater ambitions than the rest of his family and like so many others, he seemed impressed by financial wealth.

In 1879 at the age of 15 Lee was offered employment at

Emma Keyse's house, the Glen, is no longer part of this scene at Babbacombe, which has otherwise hardly changed since her violent death in 1884.

The Glen, the home of Miss Emma Keyse, who at one time had been maid to Her Majesty Queen Victoria. Miss Keyse was a greatly respected member of Babbacombe society. She had worked hard all of her life and was now in the position where she could profit from her years of service. Her idyllic home was situated within yards of Babbacombe beach and sat proudly at the foot of woodland which rose onto the cliffs. Miss Keyse also employed a cook by the name of Elizabeth Harris, who was half-sister to Lee, and two servants – Eliza Neck who had served at The Glen for almost half a century and Jane Neck. Her household staff described her as a very strict and serious lady. John Lee lasted just twelve months at The Glen, much preferring the opportunities of life on the open sea with the Navy.

In 1882 Lee was invalided out of the service, having contracted pneumonia and being unable to perform his duties at sea. He therefore returned to the Babbacombe district where in the space of a few weeks he served in three separate occupations; the first a junior position at the Yacht Club Hotel, then a porter at Torre station, and finally a post with a Colonel Brownlow. It was in this last position that Lee was caught in the act of stealing. Whether this was his first attempt is not clear, but Lee had seemingly suffered a dramatic change of character during his term in the Navy. The resulting prosecution meant a sentence of six months imprisonment in Exeter prison from July 1883 to January 1884. It was at this point that Lee's half-sister, Elizabeth Harris explained to her employer the predicament her half-brother was in. Emma Keyse felt sympathy for Lee and once more offered him employment at her home, perhaps in the hope that she could reform him.

For a period of three months or so everything at The Glen seemed rosy. Lee, the only man at the house, worked hard and appeared to be a conscientious fellow; his 68 year old employer was more than pleased with him. But all good things come to an end and so did Lee's apparent enthusiasm and interest in his work. He began to do less about the house and had a tendency to avoid work when he could, a fact which did not go unnoticed by Miss Keyse who duly spoke to him about it. Lee failed to improve his ways and so by the October of 1884 Emma Keyse was forced to take more concerted action. She hardly wanted to turn him out onto the streets as this would be against her principles and so she opted for a different course of action, one that was to prove fatal. She reduced Lee's wages from two shillings and sixpence per week to two shillings, a fact which infuriated him but left him with little in the way of alternatives. Any sensible adult would of course have striven to attain a higher standard of work but not John Lee, he simply continued to deliberately avoid performing tasks. It would appear that he felt quite militant about the whole affair – if he was reduced to less wages then quite simply he could not be expected to carry out as much work. With the benefit of hindsight it is quite easy to realise the volatile atmosphere which was brewing within The Glen, though perhaps at the time this was not so evident to its inhabitants.

The situation deteriorated until the night of Saturday 15th November 1884, when Emma Keyse received her usual cup of cocoa from her maid, Jane Neck, who then went to her quarters. It was around 12.40 am and all was peaceful, the house had been secured and the staff had all gone to bed. Emma Keyse changed into her nightgown and put on a small woollen jacket to keep out the cold of the November night air. Sometime after this she ventured into the hall where she was confronted by her killer, who bludgeoned her skull and slit her throat with such vigour that the knife inflicted notches upon her vertebrae. As if such atrocities were not sufficient, the killer then dragged her body from the hall and into the dining room where he made an attempt to burn it. Still not satisfied, various other fires were started within the house.

Elizabeth Harris was awakened by the distinct odour of smoke sometime around 3 to 4 am. She immediately awoke Jane and Eliza Neck, and then made her way downstairs and entered the dining room where she saw the partially charred remains of her employer laid upon the floor, surrounded by smouldering newspapers which had been saturated with paraffin. John Lee then appeared, allegedly awoken by the smoke and commotion. He was instructed to go at once to the nearby Carey Arms public house and raise the alarm, but instead Lee preferred to assist the Neck sisters clamber down the stairs and a number of minutes passed before he left the house to raise the alarm. With this done it was not too long before the police arrived on the scene and official investigations into the murder commenced.

Each of the household staff was interviewed as to what they were doing at the time of the fire and immediately before they retired to bed; all apparently supplied reasonable explanations. A search of the house was made in order to ascertain just how the attacker had gained entry. There were no signs of forced entry, which was quite mystifying as the house had been secured before everyone had retired that evening. This of course meant one thing, the killer must still be within the house and if it was no intruder then it had to be one of the staff. The investigating police officers must have felt quite confident that this killer would be brought to justice. Close to John Lee's quarters the police found a bloodstained hatchet, within a drawer in the pantry they found a bloodstained knife which was the property of John Lee, also within the pantry was an old oil can which smelled very strongly of paraffin. A search of John Lee's quarters revealed a bloodstained pair of trousers from which a strong aroma of paraffin emanated. Blood was even found upon Jane Neck's nightgown in close proximity to where Lee had assisted her down the stairs! John Lee was arrested for murder.

During subsequent questioning, Lee attempted to explain that he was not guilty of the crime, claiming that he and Emma Keyse were best of friends, but such claims were easily disproved by the other household staff and Lee was charged with murder. Emma Keyse was buried locally just five days after her murder. The whole community mourned her death and there was much animosity towards John Lee, who consistently denied his guilt and to everyone's surprise displayed little or no emotion at the serious allegation being made against him. Indeed for much of the time he seemed unaware of the seriousness of his situation. The usual unsubstantiated rumours connected with acts of murder began to circulate around the district, to such an extent that at least one newspaper claimed that more than one person was involved in the crime. The police ignored all such suggestions and continued in their quest for evidence to prove Lee's guilt. The inquest into Emma Keyse's death was held at St Marychurch and concluded on the 28th November with the predictable verdict of 'Wilful murder' with John Henry George Lee named as the murderer, and on the 12th day of December 1884, just ten months since his previous term of imprisonment, Lee returned to Exeter prison to await trial.

The trial commenced on the first day of February 1885 at Exeter, Mr Justice Manisty the presiding Assizes judge. Surprisingly, the defence offered an alternative solution to the crime as Lee pleaded not guilty. It was purported that Elizabeth Harris, who was pregnant at the time, had been entertaining her boyfriend at The Glen on the night in question, and that it was he who had murdered Emma Keyse and not Lee. The jury listened intently to the facts produced in court and when required took just 40 minutes to find Lee guilty of murder. On the 4th February 1885 Mr Justice Manisty passed the death sentence upon John Lee, stating that it was one of the most barbarous murders to have been

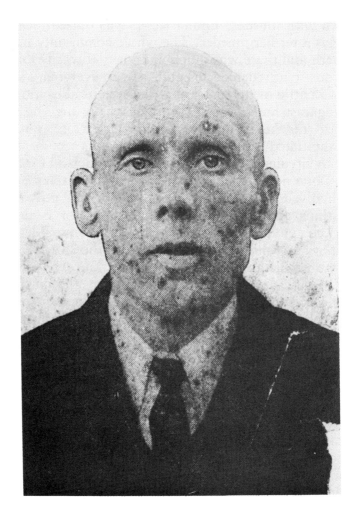

John 'Babbacombe' Lee, sentenced to hang for the murder of Emma Keyse.

committed. He further commented upon Lee's apparent calm and aloof state throughout the trial, which was not beyond the behaviour of such a malicious character and killer such as Lee. In reply to this accusation Lee retorted: 'The reason, my lord, why I am so calm and collected is because I trust in my Lord, and He knows I am innocent.' The execution was set for 23rd February and Lee was led away from the drama of the courtroom and taken back to Exeter prison where he was placed in the condemned cell.

During his short term of detention within the condemned cell of Exeter prison, Lee remained calm and unmoved. He continued to claim his innocence and held no obvious fears about his forthcoming execution. Monday 23rd February, the day of Lee's execution, arrived all too quickly for the condemned man. The scaffold had been erected in a small shed located in the north-east wing of the prison; the shed normally accommodated prisoners' vans and was of brick construction. A beam ran across the interior of the shed from which the hangman's rope was fastened; immediately beneath the rope was the trap door, suspended some eleven feet above the pit into which the condemned prisoner was dropped with considerable force. Thus the individual about to suffer execution did not have to ascend onto the gallows platform, but simply walked into the building and stood upon the trap door – not that any of this made any difference to the eventual outcome, but it was certainly deemed to be of some psychological benefit and apparently maintained some dignity and calm among those condemned as they entered the shed.

The executioner, James Berry, was proclaimed as being 'England's best'. A short time before 8 am on the morning of the execution he entered the condemned man's cell and pinioned him. Some ten journalists took up their official positions in the main corridor of the prison at a location which Lee had to pass en route to the scaffold. Within seconds the procession passed through the corridor led by the chief warder (Mr Rainford). Next came the chaplain and the schoolmaster followed by the pinioned Lee who was accompanied by two prison warders, one at each side. James Berry, the executioner, brought up the rear, following the governor and a group of other warders. The prison bell rang its clanging chime of doom. Despite the air of gloom and despondency John Lee walked to the scaffold with his head held high and with apparent confidence!

Within a minute of leaving his cell John Lee was positioned on the trap door through which he was to be thrust into eternity. Those who were present claimed that Lee looked at the beam supporting the rope as though to assure himself that it was correctly fastened. Berry placed the white cap over Lee's face and assumed his position. He then drew the lever, but the trap door failed to open. He pulled the lever a second and third time in an attempt to draw the bolt but other than a grating sound and a slight movement of the door there was nothing – the scaffold had malfunctioned. The noose was removed from Lee's neck and the white cap taken away. Lee was moved off the trap door whilst Berry and several warders attempted to identify and correct the problem with the scaffold. Throughout this John Lee stood in a confident and calm manner; he seemed totally at ease with the situation, unlike the prison officials who were hurriedly attempting to resolve the matter. Before too long Lee was again made to take up position over the trap door and the usual actions carried out. Once again Berry pulled the lever. A loud click was heard but not the usual thud associated with the victim dropping through the door. Indeed, John Lee still stood upon the trap door, which yet again had not moved. Lee was taken off the scaffold as Berry and the warders chipped pieces of wood from the trap door and carried out several attempts to rectify the cause of the obstruction. Once again Lee was placed upon the trap door and once again the lever failed to remove the bolt.

Lee was again removed from the scaffold and saw the look of deep concern among those officials who had witnessed the fiasco up to that point, none more so than James Berry. Lee was taken back into the confines of the prison while a carpenter was called to attend to the trap door and further checks were made of the machinery. Amazingly, Lee was brought back for a fourth time but did not have to suffer the horrors of further despair at the doors of eternity. He was returned to his cell whilst the governor held consultations with the prison chaplain and surgeon. All agreed that Lee had already suffered horrors that no living soul could imagine!

The Under Sheriff of Devon, H.M. James, organised an immediate appointment with the Home Secretary, Sir William Harcourt and it was decided to commute the death penalty to penal servitude for life, a punishment which caused some concern among friends and relatives of Emma Keyse who felt that Lee had got away almost scot-free. The prisoner was not advised of the commutation for over 24 hours after the decision had been made, presumably because the prison officials required official notification. Rumours were rife within Babbacombe, St Marychurch and Torquay that the failure of the gallows had been contrived and that great wagers had been made to the effect that John Lee would not hang. However, these were pure supposition and no real evidence to support these claims was ever produced. Lee was held in Portland prison, Dorset. After serving 20 years he anticipated release but on 27th March 1905 he learned that the Home Secretary, Mr A. Akers-Douglas had refused this due to the fact that he had made threats of suicide and further threats to harm living persons upon his release. The case was deliberated over the next year or so and eventually John Lee was released from Portland prison on the 18th December 1907. Upon release he returned to Abbotskerswell to his mother's home. It seems that he maintained a very low profile, although he had become something of an object of curiosity in the area with many people travelling hundreds of miles to see him.

On 22nd January 1909 by a special licence Lee married Miss Jessie Augusta Bulleid, a mental nurse at Newton Abbot Workhouse, and later that same year the couple removed from Devon opting to start afresh in the county of Durham. It was not too long before the couple were on the move again, this time to London, from where in 1911 Lee emigrated to Canada as a gold prospector, leaving Jessie and two children in England. During his brief stay in London, Lee had become popular at local fairs where he was put on show as 'The Man They Could Not Hang'. Such appearances earned him substantial riches but there were many who disliked the fact that he should profit from the act of murder and he often received much abuse, which may well be the reason for him leaving England.

It is claimed that during the First World War Lee joined the Canadian Forces, and actually visited England. He was last heard of in 1922, residing in Buffalo, USA. Curiously, the following year saw a film titled *The Man They Could Not Hang – A Cinema Oratorio* shown at the Empire in

Newton Abbot. The film was a great success and in the space of one week some 54,000 people had watched it at a Cardiff cinema. Some people believe that Lee returned to England and travelled the country with the film, making a guest appearance, but there is no evidence to support such claims.

It is generally believed that John Lee died in Milwaukee USA in 1933, but as so often occurs in such circumstances there are different tales surrounding Lee in death. Some believe he actually died in Australia during the First World War, but another tale is slightly more curious and relates to a story told by a policeman who was involved in Lee's arrest and which has been passed down through the generations. If true it certainly throws doubt on accepted facts about Lee's later years. Police Constable Frederick Boughton was one of the officers called to assist in Lee's arrest in 1884. Shortly after Lee's release from Portland in 1907, Boughton met him in a local public house and the latter gave him a half crown which he was to treasure for many years. Frederick Boughton afterwards monitored the activities of John Lee and believed that he at one time managed a public house in Borough High Street, Southwark, London and later had an antiques shop in Praed Street, Paddington. Apparently during the Second World War and the blitz of London, a bomb exploded next to Lee's antiques shop and Lee was able to take cover on the ground floor of the building which collapsed around him. Rescuers rushed to the scene and Lee was pulled out by a police officer who said to him 'I'll bet that's the closest shave you have ever had in your life'. If correct, then Lee cannot have died in the USA in 1933, but once again we have only pure speculation with little supporting evidence.

Despite the fact that most persons at the time accepted that

Lee was the murderer and that the commutation of the death penalty was not of his doing, there were still some rather odd tales printed within the pages of the local press; indeed, these tales were still prominent some 52 years later. In 1890 a claim was made by two young boys who had been present at the churchyard burial of a local resident who, it was claimed, was 'a demented young man'. After the service one individual turned to a friend and was heard to say, 'Today we have buried the secret of the Babbacombe murder!' More recently a claim was made in 1936 that when Lee was released from prison he at once visited the offices of Isidore J. Carter, who had been the prosecutor for the crown at Lee's trial and had also been legal adviser to Emma Keyse. Carter had allegedly told Lee that the person he had been shielding all those years had long been deceased! The inference was that Lee had not been Emma Keyse's killer, but had played a leading role in the instigation of it.

Perhaps the most disturbing part of the legend of John Lee is the fact that the victim of his alleged crime has been all but forgotten, with most narrators discussing the reasons as to why 'Babbacombe' Lee did not drop on the scaffold. The saddest travesty of justice surely has to be that Lee believed that it was divine intervention! Berry the hangman believed that it was the fault of hinges and bolts, and one individual believes that it was a deliberate act carried out by the prisoners who erected the scaffold, using a warped plank which when pressure was applied forced the trap door to jam. We shall never know, but what is certain is that Miss Emma Keyse was brutally murdered that fateful winter's evening in 1884, and the man brought to justice for that crime was to profit from her death, despite the fact that he may have suffered for some six minutes upon faulty gallows!

THE MURDEROUS
CHIMNEY SWEEP

S OME murders defy all reason and are totally devoid of
any logic. For obvious reasons such crimes pose serious
problems for the investigating authorities, astute
questioning of suspects (should any exist) and thorough
examination of witness testimony, plus any clues left at the
scene of the crime, being all that the police have to go on.
Today's technology greatly assists matters and to be fair in
modern day terms there are few crimes of murder which
remain unsolved or at the very least unsolvable. Victorian
detectives relied more on good fortune and basic instinct to
deny a killer freedom. The latter is perhaps still the most
utilised tool a police officer possesses.

The Victorian police of Devon and other similar rural
communities were also blessed with other assets which
assisted with their enquiries, particularly the fact that so
many of the areas they policed were so far remote that
almost everyone knew everyone else's business and precise
movements. If a local person had an altercation with another
then it would very quickly become local knowledge, thus
every so often providing a motive for a crime. Similarly, if
a stranger had been seen in the locality, in most cases a first
class description would be recorded, supplying much in the

way of necessary information. It was in 1854 in a remote part of Devon that such circumstances prevailed and directed the police to their killer.

The lanes and roads surrounding Bideford are typically Devonian – narrow and winding, and in the mid 19th century they must have been similar, albeit somewhat wilder. Each large community has its share of agitators, people to be avoided at all costs, and a town the size of Bideford would have a few, some naturally troublesome, others self-imposed troublemakers. One such individual took to the lanes near Bideford in the May of 1854. He had been a chimney sweep in the town and was the son of a woman of very loose morals but with a name which could almost have been mistaken for gentry: Llewellin Garret Talmage Harvey!

It was perhaps this name which caused Llewellin so much grief, for he always attempted to live up to it. He was provided with an excellent education which added further problems and greatly assisted his false ambitions. Having received his education Llewellin soon found that life was not going to offer him instant riches, these could be obtained in one of only three ways: inheritance (of which there was no chance), hard work (which was difficult and too time consuming) and via criminal activities (this to Llewellin's mind seemed the logical alternative). He became a petty thief with an untrustworthy reputation and it appears that the chimney sweep operation was a front for his life of crime – and to be fair it offered an ideal cover to identify good properties for future burglaries. Llewellin, however, failed at most things he attempted and his life reached the point where he held a deep dislike and mistrust of everyone. This was undoubtedly brought about by his own activities and disloyal actions; the fact was that no one trusted him, he had become one of those people who everyone chose to avoid!

Some time around the 14th/15th May 1854 Llewellin decided that he had taken about as much as he could from the people residing in the area where he lived and he openly stated that it was his intention to murder someone. He intended to do someone, anyone, serious harm. Nobody took his claim seriously, it could hardly be termed a threat as no one felt that it would be carried out.

In the afternoon of 15th May Mary Allen was walking along the country lanes leading to Little Torrington when she happened upon Llewellin sat on a grassy bank close to Stibb Cross. Mary found herself the object of his attention and Llewellin sprang up from his seated position and suggested to her that he should walk with her. Mary Allen was more than a little frightened by this and as is always the case, her perceptions were alerted to the possibility of danger and she noticed the handle of a knife or some similar object protruding from the corner of his pocket. With some courage, Mary proceeded to humour him before hurrying off, leaving Llewellin behind.

The next day, unaware of anything out of the ordinary, a labourer was walking along the Little Torrington and Langtree Week road and was just passing Croft Hill when he heard strange murmurs coming from a nearby field. Curious as to the source of the noise the man pulled aside the thick hedgerow in order to see into the hidden field. The sight which greeted him must have shocked him to his very foundations; there lay the body of a young woman, her head saturated in blood from the wounds inflicted upon her, and from the position of the body it seemed probable that some type of sexual encounter had taken place. The police were summoned and the girl was taken to a nearby hospital.

It was not too long before she was identified as 20 year old Mary Richards. Mary regained consciousness but remained in a critical state. She gave a brief description of her assailant, notably that he wore sandy coloured whiskers. It was not too long before the comments made by Llewellin Garret Talmage Harvey came to the notice of the police and he was at once apprehended, but denied any involvement in the attack. The police were faced with an immediate problem; Mary Richards described her attacker as wearing sandy whiskers, Llewellin Harvey wore no such whiskers at the time of arrest and he denied ever wearing them! Witness testimony did little to assist matters. Some claimed that Harvey did wear whiskers and others denied the same, while many were unsure that he could commit such a crime and felt that he was a harmless imbecile. With Mary Richards hovering at death's door the decision was taken to bring together victim and suspected attacker. Mary at once identified Harvey as her attacker. Mary explained that she had been sexually abused during the attack and was convinced that despite the obvious physical disguises worn by the accused, she was certain that it was him.

Mary Allen also came forward and described her encounter with Llewellin Harvey the day prior to the attack upon Mary Richards, while another witness told how he had been seen in the Croft Hill area on the 16th of May. On 30th May 1854 Mary Richards died as a result of the injuries sustained during the attack; the poor young girl had suffered at the hands of a monster, a young life destroyed in a moment of madness.

Llewellin Garret Talmage Harvey was tried and found guilty of murder and sentenced to death. Prior to his execution he confessed to the crime and gave as his reasons the problems he had faced all of his life in attempting to live up to his grandiose name.

A pointless crime which served no purpose; today many people suffer greatly from attempting to live up to a lifestyle which they can ill afford, thankfully most of them will not resort to murder.

THE MURDER AT
JACOB'S WELL

N ESTLED in the north-eastern corner of Dartmoor is
the town of Moretonhampstead, which by
comparison with its neighbours is a very large
community. There cannot be many who visit the town who
know that it is directly associated with the county's most
famous crime of murder and a serious miscarriage of justice.

Jonathan May was a 48 year old farmer of some affluence
within the communities of Moretonhampstead and
Dunsford, which were close to his home at Sowton Barton.
Like all other landowners Jonathan May employed a small
number of staff to carry out labouring duties and in general
most of May's workforce were content with their employer.

At some point in 1834 Jonathan May was doing his
rounds, visiting his staff and passing words of advice and
instructions to them. He met with George Avery and told
him to gather some firewood logs and to take them up to his
house as soon as possible. George Avery was a well built
young man and was known to possess more than a modicum
of skill in the sport of wrestling, so the removal of the logs
would have caused him few, if any, problems. Jonathan May
then left and set off on horseback to Exeter, but for reasons
known only to himself he soon turned back and returned to

his estate. It would appear that May anticipated something transpiring that day for he at once went to the cottage where Avery resided and caught him unloading the logs there, the obvious inference being that Avery was stealing part of the load! May was furious. He at once sacked Avery and told him to leave the cottage as soon as possible, intimating that he would not provide a reference for future employment and would in fact broadcast the fact that he was dishonest. In short, George Avery's reputation was destroyed and life offered him little should he choose to remain in the area. Avery packed his belongings and immediately departed but not before he had threatened to get even with Jonathan May.

During the months which followed, George Avery travelled all over England and earned paltry sums from his wrestling skills. He took to visiting country fairs and profited greatly from wagers placed upon him in the wrestling ring at such venues. Eventually, in July 1835, George Avery returned to Moretonhampstead for its annual fair. He had with him a young girl aged 22 by the name of Elizabeth Harris, and also there were two friends whom he had met upon his travels. Both bore interesting nicknames, namely 'Buckingham Joe' and 'Dick Turpin'. Neither of these men were of a decent character and one can well imagine that they were expert thieves.

The Moretonhampstead fair that year was a great success. Cattle and other livestock were traded, with most parties being satisfied that they had made profitable transactions, while the merry sound of musicians filled the air and the summer sun shone down upon the active throng. Among those who had been to the fair was Jonathan May. He had sold a number of cattle from his stock and elected to visit the White Hart Inn to celebrate his riches. Now whether it was

The White Hart inn, Moretonhampstead, on the site of the original inn where Jonathan May paraded his wealth and sealed his fate.

just plain stupidity or over-zealous consumption of alcohol which affected his judgement one cannot say, but May acted in a most foolhardy manner once within the inn. In front of a large crowd he produced from his pockets somewhere in the region of £80 in gold and note form, the product of an excellent day at the sales.

May remained in the inn until some time shortly after 10 pm when he mounted his horse and set off along the Exeter road en route for his home. A short while later residents of Moretonhampstead were surprised to see May's horse return to the town unaccompanied. A search of the town area was carried out but no trace of Jonathan May could be found and so it was decided by a few that they would search May's route home in case he had fallen from his mount and injured himself. About one mile from the town close to Jacob's Well, the unconscious body of Jonathan May was found. He had suffered a severe beating and was almost unrecognisable. Opposite the place of the attack it was evident that two persons had made good their escape via a field of barley as their tracks disappeared into the sunset.

May was taken back to the White Hart Inn at Moretonhampstead whilst a number of men remained at the scene and made a quick search for the perpetrators of the sickening attack; although with the fading light the search was only a half-hearted effort and thus terminated fairly quickly. Jonathan May never recovered from his wounds and died shortly after his arrival at the White Hart. The local constable was summoned and the enquiries commenced and brought to light a number of suspects, all of whom were questioned as to their movements on that night of 16th July.

It was not too long before it was realised that George Avery had returned to the town and there were many who recalled his parting threat to Jonathan May the previous year when he had been sacked. This was sufficient reason for the constable to place Avery and his girlfriend, Elizabeth Harris, under arrest on suspicion of murder. The pair were taken before magistrates before being secured in Exeter gaol whilst further evidence was obtained. The police were 'assisted' in their investigation and enquiries by a local solicitor by the name of Woolland Harvey, whom it appears fancied himself as something of an amateur detective.

Enquiries led the investigating authorities to the lodging house where George Avery had been staying on the night in question, and the family who lived there told how Avery had returned home early. When he came in he had asked what the time was and they had advised him that it was eight o'clock. He had then gone to bed and at ten o'clock had once again come downstairs and asked what the time was. Other witnesses from the White Hart Inn told a similar story of how Avery had said that he was too tired and had retired early from the merrymaking. With such overwhelming evidence to support his plea of innocence there was little the authorities could proffer to suggest burden of guilt and so Avery and Harris were released after being held for about one month.

Woolland Harvey's amateur efforts were somewhat subdued, though he regularly accosted the criminal element, questioning them as to their whereabouts on the night of the murder. Such inquisitiveness caused him a great amount of grief and he was regularly threatened and felt so oppressed that he purchased himself a pistol which he carried with him at all times. It is said that on one occasion the pistol discharged in his pocket and wounded him in his thigh. Despite such setbacks he maintained his interest in the case and refused to let it drop.

Months passed, and slowly the case dropped from public memory until the following year when Woolland Harvey received a message from the chaplain of Dorchester gaol who explained that a prisoner there had been exercising with other inmates when he spoke of nefarious activities with a chap called 'Turpin'. Together, it was said, the two men had battered and robbed a farmer in Devonshire. Upon receipt of the letter Harvey set out for Dorchester where he made further enquiries into the matter and in consequence of these searched the prisoners' dwellings, in which he found a watch and other personal items allegedly belonging to Jonathan May! The prisoner was identified as 'Buckingham Joe' or 'Buckingham Joe Oliver', whose real identity was Joseph Infield, a young man of about 20 years of age. The 'Buckingham' derived from the fact that he was raised there and had strong ties with the town. Without further delay Joseph Infield was brought to Exeter gaol for further questioning.

Quite by chance, George Avery and Elizabeth Harris were also resident in Exeter gaol at the time when Joseph Infield was brought there. Avery and Harris had been tried and found guilty of separate offences; Avery of highway robbery and Harris of theft, and as a result the pair were awaiting transportation to Australia. The news of the infernal ramblings of Infield spread through the gaol and eventually came to the ears of George Avery. Once again he found himself the centre of speculation and gossip, as fellow prisoners were also of the opinion that he was worthy of suspicion and connected with the crime. Further news leaked that a £100 reward had been posted and a free pardon was offered to any person supplying information which would lead to the arrest of Jonathan May's killer(s).

Elizabeth Harris requested to speak with the governor of the gaol and was duly granted an audience with him, during which she confessed to knowing more about the murder than she had previously admitted. She claimed that she had actually witnessed the murder and identified the killers as two men known to her as 'Buckingham Joe' and 'Dick Turpin'. Infield was brought before her and she unhesitatingly identified him as the man she saw kill

Jonathan May; further to this she gave an excellent description of the man she knew as 'Dick Turpin'. And so the search for the mysterious 'Turpin' commenced, though it should be remembered that this particular Turpin was not the one whose exploits have been carved into the history of the English highwayman.

At about the same time as the investigation into the Devon murder was making progress, another felon by the name of Edmund Galley was an inmate of Cold Bath Fields prison in London, charged with vagrancy. Galley appeared to be older than his claimed 24 years and he had previously worked in Dartford, Kent as an ostler, though he also tended a number of gardens and was generally capable of turning his hand to anything. More provokingly he was also known to occasionally use the name Dick Turpin! Without further delay Edmund Galley was sent to Exeter where he was taken before Elizabeth Harris. The identification was not as straightforward as everyone had hoped, for in her initial description she described 'Turpin' as well built with bushy whiskers; Edmund Galley was not what one could call 'well built', neither did he wear whiskers! It was explained to Harris that he could well have shaved his whiskers off and that she should take a long close look at the man before her. This she did and eventually she agreed that this suspect was indeed the man she saw with 'Buckingham Joe' murdering Jonathan May.

The authorities were not slow in announcing that they had two suspects under arrest for the murder at Jacob's Well the previous year and as was, and still is, usual in such cases, a number of witnesses came forward with further evidence, a large proportion of whom were womenfolk who visited many fairs all over England. All identified Joseph Infield as a travelling man who had been at the fair in Moretonhampstead in 1835, likewise the identification of Edmund Galley was almost unanimous until a woman by the name of Charlotte Clarke intervened. She had no qualms about identifying Infield but denied knowing Galley, the man she knew as 'Turpin' was totally different, a good looking man and possessing a fine set of teeth, though distinctively one of his front teeth was missing. Edmund Galley was hardly good looking and possessed all of his front teeth. Despite this, Galley was charged as co-defendant with Infield for the murder of Jonathan May, Elizabeth Harris received her free pardon and the case appeared to be straightforward – but nothing in a murder case can be accepted as being a formality.

Elizabeth Harris, now a free woman, was able to give evidence at the trial, which commenced at Exeter on the 28th July 1836 with Mr Justice Williams presiding over affairs. Joseph Infield was extremely fortunate to be able to afford the luxury of a defence counsel, Edmund Galley meanwhile had no one to offer his side of the story. Elizabeth Harris took her place in the witness stand and told the court that she was born in Burrington, Devon and had left home at the tender age of 13 years, since when she had travelled England with a number of different men friends. She had known George Avery for over a year and during this time they had been lovers. Harris, who gave her testimony in a cool and deliberate manner, further explained that she had refrained from telling the truth through fear of retribution but eventually her conscience had got the better of her. On the evening of the crime she had suspected 'Buckingham Joe' and 'Turpin' of plotting something and had followed them, hiding in the hedgerow as she went along. Eventually she saw Mr May and then heard the sound of blows. There was sufficient light for her to instantly recognise his assailants as the two men standing in the dock; of the identity of Edmund Galley she had no doubt, it was the man she had seen at numerous fairs, 'Dick Turpin'! The jury took just ten minutes to decide that both prisoners were guilty.

Upon hearing the judgement Joseph Infield shouted: 'My lord, do not, I hope you will not condemn an innocent man. The man by my side is innocent, as innocent as you are. I never saw him in my life until I saw him in the gaol, I was there but this man was not. The man who did this is also known as 'Turpin'. My lord, the man with me at the time is a good looking man, about an inch taller than I am and no more like this man than this candle. The man, my lord, was not at all like this man.'

Edmund Galley now added his plea. 'My lord, I am innocent, but God will forgive you if you cause me to suffer innocently. If I had money I could prove that I was not in Devonshire. The witnesses, my lord, have all sworn falsely against me, but I hope God will forgive them all. I was never in this county before in my life.'

Once again Joseph Infield spoke: 'I hope, my lord, that you will not hang an innocent man. I declare before God that this man was not with me. He was never with me in all my life. The evidence, my lord, is false. The witnesses were all deceived. He is not the man, he is not like the man.'

Galley's response to this was short and clear: 'I never saw this man, my lord and ladies in this court, never until I saw him in prison. All men for such offences ought to die, but I am an innocent.'

The trial judge then spoke to Galley and displayed something in the way of sympathy, as he invited him to question the witnesses who had in his words 'sworn falsely against him', but despite this opportunity Galley refrained from any further cross examination of witnesses, claiming that he knew nothing of the people concerned as he had never been to Devonshire before, thus he did not know what to ask. It is only when one reasons upon this last point that it is possible to see that Galley was unable to save himself from a miscarriage of justice; if he had not been in Devon before then how could he attempt to question witnesses as to his movements! The judge passed the death sentence upon both men and the trial ended, but it was far from a satisfactory conclusion. Many people present felt that Edmund Galley had been the victim of mistaken identity. A certain Mr Alexander Cockburn took up the case and recruited several persons who also felt strongly about Galley's innocence, and though they had little time to research Galley's claims, they almost immediately visited both men in Exeter gaol.

Galley was demented when the men visited him, the pressures of the trial having caused him great suffering to the extent that he could not recall where he was and what he was doing on the night of 16th July 1835. It was to be two or three days before Galley could recount his movements with any accuracy, but then with such intricate detail that if he was speaking the truth the team of private investigators would stand every chance of proving his innocence. Galley told the men that he was at Dartford fair that same date, where a coconut stall had been overturned and he helped to retrieve some of the scattered coconuts. Furthermore, he had a fight with a man over some money; he lost the fight but a while later won it back by virtue of a card trick. He identified three other men who knew of his presence at the Dartford fair; the three men were contacted by letter and duly confirmed what Galley said. The Dartford fair was similarly confirmed as taking place on the same day as the murder of Jonathan May. The evidence heard at the trial therefore had to be incorrect.

The Home Office received notification of the findings in favour of Edmund Galley and Sir Frederick Roe, the then Chief Magistrate of Bow Street visited Dartford to carry out his own investigation into Galley's alibi, which was very soon established. Galley was reprieved on a temporary basis until the 26th August 1836. The trial judge Mr Justice Williams was adamant that Galley had received a fair trial and that the evidence at the time supported his guilt, the inference being that he disbelieved the new evidence as being promulgated as a result of the official judgement against Galley! In the meantime Joseph Infield, alias 'Buckingham Joe Oliver' was executed before a very large crowd at the entrance to Exeter gaol on 12th August 1836. As he stood on the gallows he confessed his guilt and told the officials who were gathered that the real identity of the 'Turpin' who took part in the murder of Jonathan May was a man named Longley; it was he who had killed Jonathan May after Infield pulled him from his horse, and later when the two robbers/murderers fought over their illegally obtained rewards, Longley who was bigger and stronger won and took the riches. His last words upon the gallows were that he was guilty, but that the other man who stood trial with him was innocent.

It was not too long before a man named Longley came to light, incarcerated in Bath prison. The Devonshire authorities received notification of Longley's whereabouts but stubbornly refused to act upon the allegations made against him and he was never brought to account upon the matter. Meanwhile Edmund Galley was then moved to the prison hulks at Woolwich; he was placed upon the *Ganymede* and suffered the indignity of having all of his facial and head hair removed. Despite this, he was recognised by at least four other prisoners who knew him of old, and more importantly, they were men who claimed that they remembered him being at Dartford fair on the day of Jonathan May's murder! Were the authorities really attempting to undermine his claim of innocence and to change his appearance so that these men would not recognise him? It seems quite probable, as still they refused to grant him a pardon, even though the evidence of his innocence was regarded as overwhelming. Further reprieves were granted and Galley was held on the hulks until 1839 when he was transported to Australia.

With Galley out of the way one could expect public interest to dwindle, but this was not the case. Various letters were passed to the Home Secretary appealing for Galley's release, most were ignored and the rest were met with refusals to look at new evidence. This continued until around 1877 when Alexander Cockburn, who by this time was Lord Chief Justice, wrote to the Home Secretary, Mr Cross identifying the evidence in Galley's favour and demanding that he receive an official pardon. The Home Secretary took a year to reply, and then he used the excuse that he felt it unjustifiable to over-rule the decision of the trial judge, the then Home Secretary and the Lord Chief Justice of the time. Various letters continued to be published in many provincial newspapers, each outlining the apparent miscarriage of justice carried out against Galley.

In May 1879 the MP for Warwick, Sir Eardley Wilmot

requested that the Home Secretary lay documents at the disposal of members of the House of Commons in order that the full facts of the case could be read and identified. Once again the Home Secretary refused to be drawn. The momentum of interest was gathering and was at full swing by 1879, by which time many people were demanding to know why Galley had not received a pardon. The Mayor, Bishop and Dean of Exeter signed a petition which contained some 2,000 signatures and was estimated to be about 30 yards long, demanding a pardon, and the people of Plymouth submitted a similar document. It seemed that the only person who deemed Galley to be guilty was the Home Secretary, Mr Cross.

Defiantly, Sir Eardley Wilmot refused to allow Cross to get away with such ignorance and on 25th July 1879 in the House of Commons he moved that: 'The innocence of Edmund Galley of the crime of which he was convicted at Exeter in 1836 has been established beyond all reasonable doubt'. He further stated that it was hoped that Her Majesty would graciously grant a free pardon to Galley who was still in Australia. His plea received a warm reception, but not from Cross who opposed the motion and the scene was set for a serious debate upon which rested the reputations of a number of eminent authorities. Eventually Cross was told quite directly that should he continue to oppose the motion in such a vigorous manner then he could find himself in the minority, thus forcing his resignation. The motion was eventually carried with a large majority. It had taken 43 years, but Edmund Galley was eventually granted his pardon; he further received the sum of £2,000 for his suffering!

There is one final curious twist to this case, and one which has caused much speculation over the years. It is claimed that upon the gallows Joseph Infield dropped a red handkerchief. Outwardly there seems little suspicious about such an act, however it was an old custom of reassuring someone in the crowd that the condemned person had not betrayed them. The question therefore has to be, who was Infield protecting? It could not be Longley as Infield had told his captors of his identity, the only other person who could be suspected was George Avery. It must be remembered that Avery had sworn revenge upon Jonathan May and he had provided himself with a perfect alibi by retiring early to his lodgings and bringing the time to his hosts' attention on two separate occasions. It is more than probable that George Avery persuaded Infield and Longley to kill May, perhaps some payment being made by virtue of the rewards gleaned from success in the wrestling ring. Longley was never tried for the murder, though he too was transported to Australia for other crimes, where he changed his name and began a new life, though his memories must have haunted him until the day he died. Again, can we really put any blame upon him when he confessed to the crime, but was not interviewed by the naive Victorian authorities who could not admit error! Victims and assailants are many in this case, I will leave it to the reader to decide just who was who!

In Dunsford churchyard can be seen the memorial stone of the initial victim of this crime. It reads:

'Erected to the memory of Jonathan May of Sowton Barton in this parish who was murdered as he was returning from Moreton fair about ten o'clock on the evening of the 16th July 1835. Aged 48 years.'

MURDERED ON
DUTY

THE unlawful killing of police officers in the execution
of their duty has occurred since the inception of the
'New Police' in 1829, when it took less than twelve
months before the first officer was murdered. His death was
dismissed as over zealousness on his part with no perpetrator
being brought to justice! Thankfully, although records show
that police officers have been killed on duty within the
county of Devon, they number but a few. None was so
gruesome or callous as that which occurred in 1938 in the
tranquil surroundings of Whimple, situated a few miles
north-east of Exeter in peaceful pastures.

Police Constable No 160 John Tremlett Potter was the
archetypal police officer of the 1930s to the 1950s, firm but
fair with lots of commonsense which inevitably earned him
great respect from villains and colleagues alike. His senior
officers were full of praise for Potter, who was extremely conscientious, though this trait got him into trouble with his wife
who suffered greatly due to her husband's love of his job. The
crime rate in Whimple in 1938 was not great, indeed Potter
had combated much of it and more or less knew every local
rogue or villain within the community; he also knew most of
their trademarks and movements during the hours of darkness.

John Potter lived with his wife and 18 year old son, William Henry, in the old police cottage in Whimple, where the whole family were a welcome part of the community. William Potter worked at the nearby Whiteway Cyder Company where, very much in the image of his father, he was a good loyal worker, well respected by his friends and employers. The family took part in or initiated much village activity and were always keen and willing to assist. As such Constable Potter was the cornerstone of the community, exactly what the community required and a good foundation for any police officer.

Like all good officers, Potter had his contacts who would supply the odd snippet of information relating to possible crimes or offenders within the area. His informants were discreet and generally accurate, hence Potter's excellent clear-up rate, yet news had reached him of some petty pilfering at the premises of Whiteway Cyder Company Limited, where his son worked. William Henry knew little of the thieving and his father, quite rightly, never attempted to coerce information from him. John Potter spent much of his off duty time attempting to gather information upon the thefts from the factory, which were a serious source of concern to him. He kept his ear to the ground and maintained discreet observation in his off duty time, but for all this he drew a blank. It seemed that no one in Whimple or the surrounding area knew anything about the crimes. It may have struck Potter that criminals from outside the district were travelling in and committing the crimes and escaping by virtue of the railway line, which was situated next to the factory, but whatever his opinion he was for the first time in his career at a total loss as to the identity of possible suspects.

On 17th January 1938 Potter was rostered to work a split shift, the second part of which was between 8 pm and midnight, but being keen to maintain observation upon the cider factory, Potter left his home at around 7 pm. He returned at around 7.30 pm and remained at home until his official duty commencement time of 8 pm, when he told his wife that he would have a walk to Knowle Cross and return home for his supper at some time around 9.30 pm. Potter collected his plated torch but left behind his truncheon and handcuffs, obviously in the belief that he was not going to encounter any problems prior to his return. His wife knew only too well that he would not have forgotten to take these with him if he felt he would require them, hence she had no worries as he set off along his usual beat. As 9.30 pm came and went, Mrs Potter was a little concerned that her husband had not returned home for his supper, but presumed that he had been called to attend an incident elsewhere and had been unable to get home. William Potter agreed with his mother's conclusions and so the pair retired to their beds in the belief that he would return home shortly after midnight at the end of duty.

John Potter did not return home at the anticipated time and Mrs Potter began to grow a little concerned. Eventually, by 3 am she had decided that something was wrong, her husband had never before failed to notify her if he was working late, and she decided to awaken William and to contact the local police sergeant at Ottery St Mary.

When the telephone rang shortly after 3 am that fateful morning Sergeant Abrahams of Ottery St Mary cannot have had any idea of what he was to be told. Mrs Potter was obviously upset and expressed her concerns to the officer, who at once agreed to come over to Whimple and to carry out a search of the area. He calmed the worried Mrs Potter and explained that all would be well. William Potter meanwhile, had decided that his father would probably be somewhere in the region of the Whiteway's cider factory, maintaining observation, and he at once visited the factory area and had a good look round the outside areas but could find no trace of his father. The factory closed at night and appeared to be all secure. He tried the main office door but found it locked, everything was quiet and there was not a soul in sight. With his search complete he decided that it would be best to return home and to speak with Sergeant Abrahams.

On arrival at the police house, Sergeant Abrahams, who

The derelict site of Whiteway Cyder Co. Ltd. P.C. Potter's suspicions about pilfering at the factory were confirmed when he came upon a burglary in progress.

had brought Constable Lamb along with him, asked the usual questions of Mrs Potter and her son – what was his frame of mind before leaving for work, what was his usual route on his beat, had he mentioned any particular jobs which interested him? William Potter explained about the petty thefts from the cider factory and told the officer that he had already visited there with no luck and seen nothing suspicious in the area. The two officers took William with them and drove around Whimple and surrounding districts in the hope that they would find Potter somewhere along these routes. They also visited nearby Talaton and questioned everyone whom they met as to whether they had seen Constable Potter, but on each occasion they met with a negative response. Householders were awoken and questioned, but no one had seen Potter since mid morning the previous day. By now the sergeant was beginning to grow more than a little concerned about the welfare of one of his officers. Could he have been knocked off his bicycle by a motor vehicle in one of the country lanes? A search of ditches and hedgerows was carried out but there was not a trace anywhere, in fact they could find no evidence of an accident or any other such incident.

After a few hours they returned to Whimple and carried out a systematic search of the railway yard and the exterior of the factory office areas. Once again there was nothing which could be described as suspicious in that vicinity and so they returned to the police house in the knowledge that they had to comfort the policeman's wife and identify what, if any, problems Potter was having either with his home life or professionally. Needless to say, Mrs Potter could not identify any such areas – as far as she was aware her husband was perfectly content. Sergeant Abrahams explained that the family had to maintain its normal routine and that William should attend work as usual as at that stage there was little he could do, in the meantime he would again check all the country lanes with the assistance of daylight. So each went their own way with Mrs Potter seated firmly by the telephone awaiting any information which might be forthcoming.

At 7 am Mr Ronald H.C. Whiteway, Managing Director of the cider company arrived at the factory. Being the keyholder meant he had to open the staff entrances, and as was usual he opened the main office door first. On stepping inside the building he was curious to see that his office door was open, since he always closed this before securing the premises every evening. Stepping further into the building he saw a policeman's helmet upon the floor. He switched on the light and received the fright of his life. His office was wrecked and covered in blood. Worse still was the fact that laid in the middle of the floor was his friend Police Constable John Tremlett Potter, with blood oozing from a number of gashes in his head. The scene was sickening and was one which was to stay with Ronald Whiteway for the rest of his life. Moments after his discovery William Potter arrived for work and was equally aghast at the carnage before him. Ronald Whiteway did his best to protect the boy from viewing the scene and sent him to find Sergeant Abrahams.

Somehow Constable Potter was still alive. He was transferred to the Royal Devon and Exeter hospital, while back at Whimple the hunt for his attackers began. There was not a living soul within Whimple who would have wished this upon Potter and all were equally united in their feeling of animosity towards the evil assailants, a fact which was to greatly assist the police investigation.

Sergeant Abrahams returned to Ottery St Mary and contacted police headquarters to report the attack. The matter had now become a serious enquiry and required the experienced skills of some of the county's best detective officers of the time. Detective Inspectors West and Harvey were called in and arrived in Whimple the same day, while the incident was actively monitored by the Chief Constable, Major Lyndon Henry Morris who visited the scene and spoke with Constable Potter's family, expressing his deep concern to them and the people of Whimple.

Scenes of Crime personnel visited Whiteway's factory and carried out a thorough examination of the whole area. Upon an office window they found a set of fingerprints which were lifted and retained as possible evidence, while every worker from the establishment was interviewed as to their movements on the night in question. Such interviews proved to be more than successful. Leslie George Downing, a 26 year old factory employee, married with a young family, was interviewed on the 19th of January. The fingerprints found upon the office window were positively identified as belonging to him, and he soon became chief suspect.

The detectives who spoke to Downing found him to be more than helpful, which was somewhat unusual for a criminal actively involved in the offence being investigated. Downing explained that a second man had taken part in the incident, by the name of Stanley Clarence George Martin, aged 27 years and again employed at the cider factory. Like Downing, Martin was married with a young family.

Leslie Downing related the activities of his colleague and himself on the night of 17th January, when both men had decided to break into Whiteway's in order to search for anything worth stealing. They had with them Stanley

Martin's cycle lamp. They were disappointed to find nothing worthwhile within the office areas and opted to steal a small tin of sweets, small compensation for their negative night's work. As they were leaving the factory office area via the front door they were confronted by Constable John Potter, who spoke to Stanley Martin and seemingly failed to see Downing who was behind a door. Almost immediately a violent confrontation between Potter and Martin occurred. This allowed a now frightened Downing to make his escape, unnoticed, and once outside he ran to the railway station and caught the 9.28 pm to Exeter. Downing denied any involvement in the attack upon Potter and insisted that he knew nothing else until the following morning when he spoke to Stanley Martin, who had cuts and bruises upon his face; he had explained that the 'copper' had inflicted these the night before and added that he had managed to escape being arrested. If he was speaking the truth then Leslie Downing had identified the assailant and the motive behind the attack, all that was left for the investigating detectives to do was to put these allegations to Stanley Martin in order to check his response and confirm or deny Downing's involvement in the matter.

Martin was interviewed and made little or no attempt to deny the allegations made against him, indeed he agreed with Downing's version of events almost entirely. He explained that as they were leaving the factory via the main door, Constable Potter had rushed in and grabbed hold of him, resulting in a fight. Somehow he had managed to overpower the officer and knock him to the floor. Once there he had picked up a chair and repeatedly clubbed him over the head with it. He could not explain why he continued to do so but added that Potter had wrenched his cycle lamp from his hand

and he had managed to wrench it back. Potter, whilst suffering the blows, had removed his police whistle from his pocket and was attempting to blow it, but Martin had managed to grab it from him. The police officer had refused to give up the fight but eventually succumbed to the heavy blows raining down upon him and Martin had fled, locking the front door behind him and leaving Potter unable to move upon the floor. Once outside he had thrown the police whistle away. He later took police officers to the location where he tossed it and from where it was subsequently retrieved. Martin was adamant that Leslie Downing took no part in the assault and was innocent of such charges, his loyalty to his friend most impressive considering the circumstances.

Both men were duly arrested, cautioned and charged with causing grievous bodily harm with intent to murder Constable Potter. Neither positively denied the charges made against them, but it seemed clear that Leslie Downing was innocent of the assault charge but guilty to burglary. The inquiry was all but complete, within 24 hours of the attack two prisoners had been locked up with confessions and the police officers concerned must have been fairly content until matters took a more serious turn.

John Tremlett Potter still lay in a critical state in the Royal Devon and Exeter hospital, and he remained unconscious for a further 16 days until the 2nd February, when he died as a result of the injuries sustained during the attack. Leslie Downing and Stanley Martin were now jointly charged with murder. Downing was devastated, he had had no obvious intention to kill nor any physical involvement in the attack, but was guilty by association. Stanley Martin appeared to accept the charge, in the realisation that the attack should have killed Potter outright on the night in question and it was only the police officer's resolve and determination that kept him alive for a further 16 days.

On 18th February both men were committed to trial at London's Central Criminal Court jointly charged with the murder of Police Constable John Tremlett Potter and breaking and entering the premises of Whiteway's Cyder Company Limited and stealing therefrom. The case aroused great public interest as the media proffered that Leslie Downing, although innocent of the crime of murder was in fact guilty, a correct assertion though one which was to

The gravestone of P.C. Potter, a conscientious police officer and pillar of the community.

cause great debate in a similar crime some years later. Leslie Downing had little to fear as those police officers who had investigated the crime realised his almost innocent participation in the murderous attack.

The trial commenced on 21st March 1938 before Mr Justice Hawke. The arguments and objections were debated at great length, but the case was never in any doubt – Stanley Martin had murdered Constable Potter; it was Downing's participation which caused the objections. The trial lasted five days and ended on 26th March, when the jury returned their verdicts. Stanley Martin was found 'Guilty of murder'; Leslie Downing 'Not guilty of murder but guilty of office breaking/burglary'. All that was left was for Mr Justice Hawke to pass sentence upon the men, and the court took on a solemn atmosphere as the black cap was donned by the judge who duly sentenced Stanley Martin to death. Leslie Downing was given a twelve month jail sentence.

With the trial over one would anticipate that the interest in the case would subside, but Stanley Martin appealed against the sentence, claiming that he had no actual intent to kill anyone and he had no obvious weapons upon him during the commission of the crime. Further to this, other objections were raised which caused the Home Secretary to commute the death penalty to one of life imprisonment. A possibly unsatisfactory conclusion to an evil and callous attack, as once again a convicted murderer escaped the justice he undoubtedly deserved.

The murder aroused great sympathy from the people of Devon, many of whom donated small amounts to a subscription fund started by police officers from all over the country. Within a short time some £740 had been raised for

The house built for the bereaved Potter family, paid for with
donations from the people of Devon.

the Potter family, and with a plot of land at Whimple
donated by Whiteway's, a house was built, thus supplying a
permanent residence for the family.

The death of Police Constable Number 160 Potter serves
as a solemn reminder of the challenge police officers face in
the execution of their duties. Murder is not synonymous
with large cities, it can happen almost anywhere at any time.

INDEX